FRENCH
MADE EASY
LEVEL 2

An Intermediate French Workbook
To Build Essential Vocabulary And Grammar With Ease
(French Audio Lessons Included)

LingoMastery

ISBN: 978-1-951949-89-1
Copyright © 2025 by Lingo Mastery
ALL RIGHTS RESERVED

No part of this book may be reproduced, stored in a retrieval system or transmitted in any form or by any means, electronic, mechanical, photocopying, recording, scanning, or otherwise, without prior written permission from the publisher.

The illustrations in this book were designed using images from Freepik.com.

CONTENTS

PREFACE / ABOUT THE LANGUAGE 1

STRUCTURE 2

INTRODUCTION 3

HOW TO GET THE AUDIO FILES 4

Unit 1: Relationships 6

  Chapter 1 – The Perfect Tense with *être* 7

    Exercises I 14

  Chapter 2 – Feelings, Emotions, and Moods 16

    Exercises II 21

  Chapter 3 – Useful Pronouns and Adjectives 23

    Relative Pronouns: *Que* and *Qui* 23

    The Pronoun *en* 27

    Demonstrative Articles 30

    Exercises III 33

  Chapter 4 – *Les Amis* 36

    C'est and Ce sont 36

    Direct and Indirect Complement Pronouns 38

    Exercises IV 42

  Chapter 5 – *Au Travail* 45

    The Formal You (*Vous*) 45

    Tonic Pronouns 47

    Including and Limiting 49

    Exercises V 52

Unit 2: School 56

Chapter 1 – Talking about Time 57
- What's the time, please? 57
- Time Sequences – Adverbs 59
- Expressing Duration 60
- *Aller* and the Near Future 62
- Exercises I 64

Chapter 2 – In the Classroom 67
- Obligation and Prohibition 67
- Relative Pronouns: Dont and Où 67
- Indefinite Articles 69
- School in France 70
- Exercises II 73

Chapter 3 – Evaluations 76
- Reported Speech – Present 76
- Progress Reports 78
- Pronominal Verbs 79
- Exercises III 82

Unit 3: Work 88

Chapter 1 – Job Searches and Offers 89
- The Passive Voice and Ways to Avoid It 89
- Adverbs ending in *-ment* 91
- Making Comparisons 92
- Exercises I 94

Chapter 2 – Job Interviews 97
    Perfect tense with *avoir* 97
    Open-Ended Questions 98
    Talking About Rules 100
    Exercises II 102

Chapter 3 – You're Fired! I Quit! 106
    Complex Negation 106
    Opposition and Concession 109
    Exercises III 111

Unit 4: Hobbies 114

Chapter 1 – Movies 115
    Verbs for Talking about Sequences 115
    Expressing an Opinion 116
    Exercises I 118

Chapter 2 – Sports 120
    Earlier, Later, at the Same Time 120
    Prepositions of Time 122
    Superlatives 123
    Exercises II 126

Chapter 3 – Crafting Hobbies 128
    Approximate Quantities 128
    Prepositions of Place 129
    Exercises III 132

Chapter 4 – Volunteering 135
    Present Subjunctive 135
    Discussing Certainty & Doubt 138
    Exercises IV 141

Unit 5: Memories, Wishes, and Plans 144

Chapter 1 – Memories 145
    Imperfect Tense 145
    Discussing Regrets 148
    Exercises I 150

Chapter 2 – The Future 152
    Intentions and Plans 152
    The Simple Future Tense 153
    Exercises II 155

Chapter 3 – Hopes and Dreams 157
    Conditional Tense: Overview 157
    Present Conditional 157
    Past Conditional 160
    Hopes 161
    Exercises III 163

Conclusion 166

Answer Key 167

Unit 1 167
Exercises I 167
Exercises II 168
Exercises III 169
Exercises IV 170
Exercises V 171

Unit 2 174
Exercises I 174
Exercises II 176
Exercises III 178

Unit 3 181
Exercises I 181
Exercises II 182
Exercises III 183

Unit 4 184
Exercises I 184
Exercises II 184
Exercises III 185
Exercises IV 186

Unit 5 188
Exercises I 188
Exercises II 189
Exercises III 189

PREFACE / ABOUT THE LANGUAGE

A foreign language is an essential communication tool for the modern era. French is currently the fifth most widely spoken language in the world, with approximately 320 million speakers. Studies show that French is also among the most commonly used languages on the Internet, ranking in the top five for website content. French evolved from Latin and is widely regarded as one of the world's most beautiful languages.

Many people today believe that French is in decline. Rumors of the language's demise are greatly exaggerated! While it no longer holds the same formal status in the world as it did in the 19th and early 20th centuries, French is still the second-most common language used in diplomacy and the third-most common language used in business. French is the official language in 32 countries and is the only language other than English that is spoken on every continent. Over 50 million people study French as a foreign language, making it the second most-taught foreign language behind only English.

Another common myth is that fewer and fewer people speak French. In reality, the number of French speakers is growing. In one recent five-year period, the number of French speakers increased by nearly 10%. A large majority of French speakers today are under 30 years old. Africa, the world's fastest growing region by population, is where the French language is growing fastest. The African continent is also home to almost 60% of the people who speak French daily.

The popularity of France as a tourist destination also makes French an essential language for travelers. France is consistently the most visited country in the world. Knowing a little French can go a long because the French love their language. While you may find more French people able and willing to speak English, especially in Paris and other well-known tourist destinations, a friendly *bonjour* and *merci* often means you'll get warmer service. In the countryside, and even in some shops and hotels in Paris, knowing basic French is essential to daily life.

Literature and film lovers will also know that many great works are originally created in the French language. Many more works, including some popular TV shows, feature quotes or sometimes longer exchanges in French. You may also have noticed that a lot of amazing works of art and pieces of music have titles in the French language. Translations and subtitles do not always do justice to these cultural experiences.

The goal of this workbook is to help you deepen your knowledge of this extremely popular and equally beautiful language. The lessons and exercises in this workbook should allow you to feel more confident with your French skills whatever your reason for learning.

STRUCTURE

Learning a language is always challenging, but it should also be a fun and rewarding experience. The aim of this book is to offer you a self-taught course of study that will allow you to understand French – and the culture to which it belongs – better.

This book will provide you with the linguistic, cultural, and strategic tools to communicate in French. The learning path has been carefully planned so that you can develop a more personal experience while practicing the language.

Each chapter is dedicated to a specific topic essential for becoming fluent in French. Some of them are more focused on grammar, while others are centered on useful vocabulary and practical situations, so that you will have all the tools you need to start navigating this fascinating language.

The exercises following each section are designed to reinforce what has been learned while allowing you to expand your vocabulary.

 This headphone symbol next to a paragraph or dialogue indicates that audio content is available for the corresponding section.

 This headphone with a pencil next to an exercise means that you will need to refer to the corresponding audio content to complete the exercise.

Ready to continue learning French in a fun and easy way?

Allons-y ! Let's go!

INTRODUCTION

This book does not aim to be a comprehensive guide covering everything about the French language. Building on the first book in the series, this book will help learners of French to communicate and understand more complex ideas. Throughout the book, you will find grammatical explanations, as well as exercises with everyday vocabulary and short texts on French culture.

Of course, the first rule is: **take your time** while exploring the different sections of the workbook — do not rush through them, but rather enjoy this journey into the French language.

This book is aimed at people of all ages who want to start learning French, or people who have already been studying the language and want to refresh their skills. It covers the basics of levels A2-B1 in the Common European Framework of Reference for Languages (CEFR), which means that by completing the lessons and exercises in this book you will develop the knowledge and skills to talk about your life, your daily routine, your hobbies, your job, or your school (A2) and to make and understand progressively more complex sentences (B1).

Try completing all the exercises, as they are structured not only to practice what you are learning in that section but also to consolidate words and rules throughout the whole book.

French is notorious for its difficult pronunciation, since many words are pronounced differently from how they are written. This book and its listening exercises will allow you to practice this skill.

HOW TO GET THE AUDIO FILES

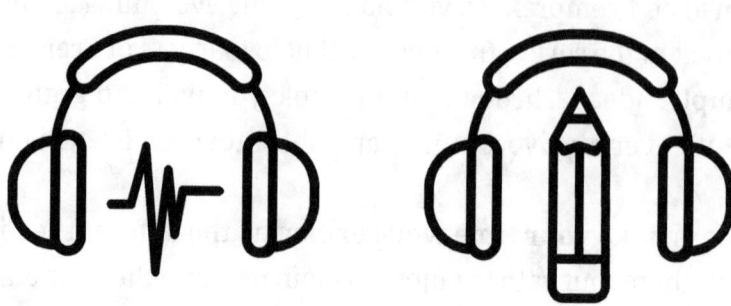

Some of the exercises throughout this book come with accompanying audio files. You can download these audio files if you head over to:
www.lingomastery.com/french-me2-audio

If you're having trouble downloading the audio, contact us at
www.lingomastery.com/contact

UNIT 1
Relationships

Unit 1 focuses on different types of relationships: romantic, family, friendships, and workplace connections. Each chapter includes grammar notes and vocabulary to help you talk about falling in or out of love, spending time with your family and friends, or interacting politely with colleagues.

CHAPTER 1
The Perfect Tense with *être*

In this chapter, we are going to focus on the perfect tense using the auxiliary verb *être*. This tense was introduced in the final chapter (Unit 5, Section 4) of the first book in this series.

Let's review the basics.

We use the French perfect tense, or *passé composé*, to speak about past actions. This one tense is used for both English-language simple past tense ('I loved it') and present perfect tense ('I have loved you for a while').

The perfect tense is called the *passé composé* in French because it is composed of three parts:

subject/pronoun + conjugated <u>auxiliary</u> verb + past participle of the <u>main</u> verb

Auxiliary Verb: *Être*

Let's start in the middle with the **auxiliary verb**. In English, the present perfect tense uses the verb "have" as the auxiliary verb, regardless of the main verb. For example, "He *has* written a book" or "The girls *have* fallen." The main verbs in these examples are "write" and "fall," and in both cases you use a conjugation of "have" to form the perfect tense.

In French, it's a little more complicated. You have two possibilities for the auxiliary verb: *avoir* and *être*. Sadly, you don't get to choose which auxiliary verb you like better. The main verb dictates the choice between *avoir* and *être*.

Step 1 with the *passé composé* is to figure out whether the main verb requires *avoir* or *être*.

For most verbs, you'll use *avoir* as the auxiliary verb. In the first English example above, to write or *écrire* is a standard "*avoir*" verb. For the sentence "He has written a book," the French translation is *"Il a écrit un livre."*

In this chapter, we focus on the *passé composé* using *être* as the auxiliary verb. You will need to memorize the list of verbs that call for *être*. A popular memory device is DR & MRS VANDERTRAMP. Each letter in the names represents a verb that requires *être*.

Here is the list:

French verb	English meaning
Devenir	to become
Revenir and	to come back
Monter	to go up / to climb
Rester	to stay
Sortir	to go out / to leave
Venir	to come
Aller	to go
Naître	to be born
Descendre	to descend / to go down
Entrer	to enter / to go in
Rentrer	to come back / to come home
Tomber	to fall
Retourner	to return / to go back
Arriver	to arrive
Mourir	to die
Partir	to leave

(**Note:** Some of these verbs can use either *avoir* or *être*, depending on their meaning and context. This chapter focuses on the most common meaning and application.)

One additional verb that uses *être* as the auxiliary verb is not included in the memory device: ***passer*** (to pass / to go by / to spend [time]). Unfortunately, there is no perfect *aide-mémoire* that includes all the *être* verbs. This group includes only 17 verbs. So, with patience and practice you will be able to memorize them even without the help of DR & MRS VANDERTRAMP.

Subject / Pronoun and Conjugation

Once you know the list of verbs that use *être* as the auxiliary verb, **Step 2** is to identify the **subject or pronoun** – the first part of the *passé composé* form. Knowing your subject or pronoun is important for two reasons.

First, you'll need to conjugate *être* in the present tense. Let's review:

Pronoun	Present tense	Meaning as <u>auxiliary</u> verb
Je	suis	I have
Tu	es	You have
Il / Elle	est	He / she has
Nous	sommes	We have
Vous	êtes	You have (plural or formal)
Ils / Elles	sont	They have (masc. / fem.)

Notice that, although *être* means "to be" when it is used as an auxiliary verb in the perfect tense, it translates to English as "have" or "has."

Past Participle

Step 2 in forming the perfect tense is to form the **past participle** of the main verb. Let's visit DR & MRS VANDERTRAMP again.

French verb	English meaning	Past participle
Devenir	to become	**devenu**
Revenir	to come back	**revenu**
Monter	to go up / to climb	monté
Rester	to stay	resté
Sortir	to go out / to leave	sorti
Venir	to come	**venu**
Aller	to go	allé
Naître	to be born	**né**
Descendre	to descend / to go down	descendu
Entrer	to enter / to go in	entré
Rentrer	to come back / to come home	rentré
Tomber	to fall	tombé
Retourner	to return / to go back	retourné
Arriver	to arrive	arrivé
Mourir	to die	**mort**
Partir	to leave	parti

You may notice that some of these verbs – the ones shown in **bold** – have irregular past participles. They do not follow the standard rules for forming the past participle from the infinitive.

The standard rules for forming the past participle are:

- verbs ending in -er .... replace -er with -é: .... parler → .... parlé
- verbs ending in -ir .... replace -ir with -i: .... finir → .... fini
- verbs ending in -re .... replace -re with -u: .... répondre → .... répondu

The French language has many irregular verbs, and five of them use *être* for the perfect tense. You will need to memorize these irregular participle forms. Thankfully, three of them are very similar: *venir, devenir,* and *revenir* become *venu, devenu,* and *revenu*.

So, we have all the components of the *passé composé* – subject / pronoun, auxiliary verb *(être)* – and past participle, but we're not done. When using *être* as the auxiliary verb, there is one final step to form the perfect tense perfectly.

Subject / Pronoun & Agreement with Participle

Step 4 requires the subject / pronoun and the past participle to have the **correct agreement**. This rule means that we have to determine whether the subject / pronoun is masculine or feminine and whether it is singular or plural.

If the subject is masculine and singular, the past participle must be masculine and singular. Masculine singular is the easiest case because you do not need to modify the standard participle.

If the subject is feminine and singular, the participle must be feminine and singular. In this case, you add an *"e"* at the end of the standard participle. For plural forms, you add an *"s"* to the standard participle for masculine subjects and an *"es"* for feminine subjects.

The table below shows each of the participle forms for the DR & MRS VANDERTRAMP verbs.

Infinitive	Standard / Masculine Singular Past Participle	Feminine Singular Past Participle	Masculine Plural Past Participle	Feminine Plural Past Participle
Devenir	devenu	devenue	devenus	devenues
Revenir	revenu	revenue	revenus	revenues
Monter	monté	montée	montés	montées
Rester	resté	restée	restés	restées
Sortir	sorti	sortie	sortis	sorties
Venir	venu	venue	venus	venues
Aller	allé	allée	allés	allées
Naître	né	née	nés	nées
Descendre	descendu	descendue	descendus	descendues
Entrer	entré	entrée	entrés	entrées
Rentrer	rentré	rentrée	rentrés	rentrées
Tomber	tombé	tombée	tombés	tombées
Retourner	retourné	retournée	retournés	retournées
Arriver	arrivé	arrivée	arrivés	arrivées
Mourir	mort	morte	morts	mortes
Partir	parti	partie	partis	parties

Putting It All Together

Now, let's look back at our earlier English example: "The girls have fallen."

Step 1: The main verb is *to fall* (*tomber*), which requires *être* as the auxiliary verb.

Step 2: "The girls" *(les filles)* are the subject of the sentence. We will use the third person plural conjugation of *être*: *sont*.

Step 3: The standard past participle of *tomber*, our main verb, is *tombé*.

Step 4: "The girls" is a feminine plural subject; so, we add an -es to the standard participle.

Final sentence: *Les filles sont tombées. Aïe !* (Ouch!)

This process will become easier with practice.

Phrases with Dr. & Mrs. Vandertramp Verbs for Romantic Relationships

French Phrase	English Meaning
Entrer en contact (avec)	to get in touch (with)
Devenir amis	to become friends
Sortir (ensemble)	to go out / to date
Rentrer au petit matin	to come home at dawn (after a night out)
Tomber amoureux/se	to fall in love
Rester ensemble	to stay together

Vocabulary for Romantic Relationships

French term	English meaning
aimer	to like, to love
l'amour	love
un baiser	a kiss
un câlin	a hug
le/la célibataire	single person
le cœur	heart
compagnon / compagne	partner
le coup de foudre	love at first sight
le couple	couple
époux(se)	spouse
fiancé(e)	fiancé(e)
la femme	wife
séduire	to flirt / to seduce
main dans la main	hand in hand
le mari	husband
passionné(e)	passionate
le petit ami	boyfriend
la petite amie	girlfriend
la relation	relationship
le rendez-vous	date (*noun*)
romantique	romantic
rompre (avec)	to break up (with)
la rupture	breakup
se disputer	to argue
se marier	to get married
se réconcilier	to reconcile
se rencontrer	to meet
se sentir bien avec quelqu'un	to feel comfortable with someone
se séparer (see also *rompre*)	to break up (implies mutual choice)
les sentiments	feelings

📝 EXERCISES I

1. **Complétez chaque phrase avec la conjugaison exacte du verbe être ou avoir.**
   Complete each sentence with the correct conjugation of être or avoir.

   a. Je _____ sortie avec lui.
   I went out with him.

   b. Tu _____ devenu une bonne amie.
   You have become a good friend.

   c. Il _____ appelé beaucoup.
   He has called a lot.

   d. Anne _____ revenue.
   She has come back.

   e. Nous _____ regardé un film ensemble.
   We watched a movie together.

   f. Vous _____ arrivés au bon moment.
   You have arrived at just the right time.

   g. Pierre et Marie _____ allés au restaurant hier soir.
   Peter and Mary went to a restaurant last night.

   h. Elles _____ tombées amoureuses de lui.
   They fell in love with him.

   i. Leur fille _____ née ce matin.
   Their daughter was born this morning.

   j. Les maris _____ restés à la maison aujourd'hui.
   The husbands have stayed home today.

2. **Traduisez chaque phrase en veillant à respecter la conjugaison et l'accord.**
   Translate each sentence, paying close attention to conjugation and agreement.

   a. Charlotte climbed the stairs (*les marches, f.*).
   _____

   b. Christophe has returned to Paris.
   _____

   c. I was born in England (*Angleterre*). (*subject is feminine*)
   _____

   d. You have gone down the wrong path (*chemin, m.*). (Use *tu*)
   _____

   e. His wife died yesterday.
   _____

   f. The man has fallen off the chair (*chaise, f.*).
   _____

   g. Their parents came home early (*tôt*).
   _____

   h. He went out with his girlfriend.
   _____

   i. We have become a happy couple.
   _____

   j. You entered without tickets (*billets, m.*). (Use *vous*)
   _____

CHAPTER 2
Feelings, Emotions, and Moods

If you've watched any French cinema, you may have noticed that the French talk about *sentiments* a lot. What might be less noticeable is the variety of verbs French speakers use to talk about their feelings, emotions, and moods. In this chapter, you'll learn how to use **être** (to be), **avoir** (to have), and the reflexive verb **se sentir** (to feel) to sound almost as sentimental as a French person.

Être

Let's start with ***être***, which probably makes the most sense to English speakers when discussing feelings. In English, "to be" is the go-to verb for expressing feelings and emotions: "I am happy." "I am afraid." "I am uncomfortable." However, in French, only one of these sentences uses *être* in the most common usage. "I am happy" → *Je suis content / contente.*

When do you use *être* to talk about feelings in French? Rest assured that the French also use **être + an adjective** as the **most common structure** to express their current feelings or emotions. For example:

- *Il est jaloux.* (He is jealous.)
- *Elles sont heureuses.* (They are happy.)

When using *être* for emotions, notice that the adjective must agree with the subject. Therefore, you will need to pay attention to the subject / pronoun both to conjugate *être* and to use the correct masculine or feminine and singular or plural form of the adjective. An example using the adjective *ravi* (delighted) is shown below.

Subject / Pronoun	Present tense	Adjective form
Je	suis	ravi (m.), ravie (f.)
Tu	es	ravi (m.), ravie (f.)
Il	est	ravi
Elle	est	ravie
Nous	sommes	ravis (m.), ravies (f.)
Vous	êtes	ravis (m.), ravies (f.)
Ils	sont	ravis
Elles	sont	ravies

The French also use *être* to express moods. Instead of using *être* + *adjective* as with feelings and emotions, the structure for moods is ***être* + *preposition* + *adjective* + *humeur*** (mood, fem.). Since *humeur* is a feminine and singular noun, the adjective must always match this form: feminine and singular.

The structure for discussing moods is similar to the English phrase: "to be in a ___ mood." There are, though, two key differences: (1) French uses *de* instead of *en* (the closest equivalent to "in"), and (2) French does not usually use the indefinite article. These examples show the two differences:

- *The girls are **in a** good mood.* → *Les filles sont **de** bonne humeur.*
- *My husband is **in a** bad mood.* → *Mon mari est **de** mauvaise humeur.*

Avoir

To express certain feelings, emotions, or physical sensations, the French language uses ***avoir*** instead of *être*. The structure is ***avoir* + noun**. This structure would literally translate as "to have + noun," but the equivalent meaning in English is "to be + adjective."

Some common expressions with *avoir* are shown here:

French phrase	English meaning
avoir peur (de)	to be afraid, scared (of)
avoir honte (de)	to be ashamed, embarrassed (of)
avoir hâte (de + infinitive)	to be excited (to do something)
avoir horreur de	to be repulsed by / to hate
avoir la pêche (slang – literal transl. "to have the peach")	to be in good spirits / to feel great
avoir le cafard (slang – literal transl. "to have the cockroach")	to be in low spirits, depressed

While *être* forms exist, using the *avoir* forms above is more common in everyday language and will make your French sound more authentic.

English	Être form	Avoir form - Preferred
to be afraid, scared	être effrayé	avoir peur
to be ashamed, embarrassed	être gêné	avoir honte
to be excited	être excité (danger !!) ⚠	avoir hâte

The *être* forms of "to be afraid" or "to be ashamed" are less commonly used, especially in spoken French, but they will not raise eyebrows. In contrast, the *être* form of "to be excited" – *être excité* – will cause a few giggles. This phrase has a second meaning that relates to sexual arousal. So it's best to avoid this expression in everyday conversation.

Se sentir

To understand this next verb, it helps to think about the difference between "I am sad" and "I feel sad." Professionals would say that "I am" is a direct expression of the feelings, while "I feel" is a description of how you perceive your feelings. In other words, when a person says, "I feel," there is some level of reflection about the feelings.

In French, **se sentir** + **adjective** is the structure to talk about internal feelings. To use this verb structure correctly, keep three key points in mind.

1. *Se sentir* is a **reflexive** verb. That means the *se* part of the verb needs to agree with the subject / pronoun: *me, te, se, nous, vous* (see below).

2. *Sentir* is an **irregular** verb. It is not conjugated like other verbs that end in -*ir* (see below).

3. The **adjective** must agree with the subject / pronoun.

Here's an example of all three points for "to feel annoyed":

Subject/ Pronoun	Reflexive pronoun	Present tense	Adjective form
Je	me	sens	contrarié (m.), contrariée (f.)
Tu	te	sens	contrarié (m.), contrariée (f.)
Il	se	sent	contrarié
Elle	se	sent	contrariée
Nous	nous	sentons	contrarié**s** (m.), contrariées (f.)
Vous	vous	sentez	contrariés (m.), contrariées (f.)
Ils	se	sentent	contrariés
Elles	se	sentent	contrariées

Common Adjectives for Talking about Feelings, Emotions, and Moods

French adjective	English meaning
Joie • heureux • content • ravi, enchanté • étonné	*Joy* • happy • content • delighted • amazed, surprised
Tristesse • malheureux • triste • déçu • seul • dévasté	*Sadness* • unhappy • sad • disappointed • lonely • heartbroken, devastated

French adjective	English meaning
Espoir • optimiste • confiant • fier • enthousiaste • reconnaissant	***Hope*** • hopeful, optimistic • confident • proud • enthusiastic • grateful
Colère et Frustration • fâché • frustré • contrarié • vexé • furieux	***Anger and Frustration*** • angry • frustrated • upset, annoyed • upset, offended • furious
Amour et Affection • amoureux • passionné • affectueux • attiré (par) • attirant • agréable • aimable • généreux	***Love and Affection*** • in love • passionate • affectionate • attracted (to) • attractive • nice, pleasant • friendly, kind • generous

EXERCISES II

1. **Pour chaque dessin, formulez une phrase pour décrire le sentiment de l'enfant.**
   For each sketch, write one sentence that describes the child's feelings.
   (If the emotion is not listed in this lesson, look it up.)

 **a.** Angry

 **e.** Disgusted

 **i.** Joyful

 **m.** Scared

 **q.** Suspicious

 **b.** Bored

 **f.** Excited

 **j.** Loved

 **n.** Shy

 **r.** Tired

 **c.** Brave

 **g.** Happy

 **k.** Proud

 **o.** Amused

 **s.** Worried

 **d.** Calm

 **h.** Jealous

 **l.** Sad

 **p.** Surprised

 **t.** Fond of eating, craving treats

a. _____

b. _____

c. _____

d. _____

e. _____

f. _____

g. _____

h. _____

i. _____

j. _____

k. _____

l. _____

m. _____

n. _____

o. _____

p. _____

q. _____

r. _____

s. _____

t. _____

French Made Easy Level 2 | Unit 1

2. Exercez-vous avec le verbe « se sentir » en faisant attention à la conjugaison et l'accord. *Practice using* se sentir, *paying careful attention to conjugation and agreement.*

a. Christine feels lonely.
   _____

b. The men feel stressed today.
   _____

c. You feel proud of your boyfriend (*petit ami*). (*tu* is feminine)
   _____

d. She feels nervous about leaving (*à l'idée de partir*).
   _____

e. I feel guilty for not helping (*de ne pas aider*).
   _____

f. My wife often feels exhausted after work.
   _____

g. We feel happy about our choice.
   _____

h. The students feel lucky to have jobs (*boulots*).
   _____

i. The women feel inspired to win.
   _____

j. You feel nostalgic in this house. (use plural)
   _____

k. They feel relieved to still love each other (*s'aimer*).
   _____

l. We feel honored to meet you.
   _____

CHAPTER 3
Useful Pronouns and Adjectives

Talking about love and relationships is not always simple. Describing our loved ones and our feelings and emotions sometimes requires adding information to basic sentences or avoiding boring repetition. In this chapter, we'll learn three techniques to help you express yourself in French with more nuance and less repetition: relative pronouns, the pronoun *en*, and demonstrative adjectives.

Relative Pronouns: *Que* and *Qui*

Let's start with the basics: *what is a relative pronoun?* You probably use them all the time without thinking about them. Relative pronouns – such as **that**, **who**, and **whom** – introduce a relative clause, meaning a phrase that adds detail about a noun in the sentence without repeating it.

It probably helps to look at a sentence that has a relative pronoun. Oh, hey – the sentence you just read is a good example. The word "that" is a relative pronoun. It introduces the relative clause: "that has a relative pronoun." In this example, the relative clause gives more information about the noun "sentence."

Before we turn to French, below are a few more examples of sentences with relative clauses in English.

- I found a restaurant **that** serves pizza.
- She loves the boy **who** lives next door to her.
- They fired the actor **whom** the fans hated.

The French language uses the relative pronouns *que* and *qui*. One big difference is both *que* and *qui* can mean "that," "who," or "whom," depending on the context. The good news is there's not a third pronoun to learn – one thing that is simpler in French than in English!

When to Use "*Que*"

You use *que* when the relative pronoun is the **direct object** of the verb in the relative clause, whether it's a person or a thing. The direct object does not perform the action in the relative clause. So, if you need to add another noun or pronoun in the relative clause to do the action, you use *que*.

Let's look at some examples:

- *Ils sont allés au restaurant. Ma sœur adore ce restaurant.* → *Ils sont allés au restaurant **que** ma sœur adore.* (They went to the restaurant. My sister loves that restaurant. → They went to the restaurant (that) my sister loves.)

- *Nous avons descendu le chemin. Un panneau a indiqué le chemin.* → *Nous avons descendu le chemin **qu'**indique le panneau.* (We went down the path. A sign indicated the path. → We took the path that the sign indicated.)

- *J'ai une tante. Mon père n'aime pas ma tante.* → *J'ai une tante **que** mon père n'aime pas.* (I have an aunt. My father doesn't like my aunt. → I have an aunt whom my father doesn't like.)

You may notice that in all of the examples, the relative clause has its own noun (*sœur, panneau, père*) that does the action in that clause.

In the second example, *que* is replaced by *qu'* to form a contraction with words that start with a vowel or a non-aspirate (mute) h (for example, *l'histoire*). You might also have noticed that the subject comes after the verb in the relative clause – "*qu'indique le panneau.*" This reversal of the order is frequent in French relative clauses. It is not a rule, but it adds poetry to the language. As you develop your ear for French, you'll be able to hear which sounds more musical – "*que le panneau indique*" ♪ or "*qu'indique le panneau.*" ♪♪♪

In the third example, *que* refers to a person (*ma tante*). Remember, in French, when used as a relative pronoun, *que* can mean "that," "who," or "whom."

When to Use *"Qui"*

You use *qui* as the relative pronoun in two situations: (1) the relative pronoun is the **subject** of the relative clause whether it's a person or a thing or (2) the relative pronoun **follows a preposition** and refers to **a person** or **people**.

Qui as Subject of Relative Clause

When the relative pronoun is the **subject** of the relative clause, it performs the action in that clause. You do not need another noun or pronoun.

Here are some examples:

Tu ne manges pas le gâteau. Le gâteau vient du supermarché. → *Tu ne manges pas le gâteau* **qui** *vient du supermarché.* (You don't eat the cake. The cake comes from the supermarket. → You don't eat the cake that comes from the supermarket.)

Ils ont des cousines. Leurs cousines sont parties vivre au Canada. → *Ils ont des cousines* **qui** *sont parties vivre au Canada.* (They have cousins. Their cousins went to live in Canada. → They have cousins who went to live in Canada.)

Notre grand-père prépare une recette de famille. Cette recette est mon plat préféré. → *Notre grand-père prépare une recette de famille* **qui** *est mon plat préféré.* (My grandfather is making a family recipe. This recipe is my favorite dish. → My grandfather is making a family recipe that is my favorite dish.)

In the above examples, you can see that the relative clause does not have a separate noun. Instead, *qui* acts as the subject of the verbs (*venir, partir, être*). Because *qui* stands in for the noun in the main clause, you need to conjugate the verb in the relative clause to agree with the main noun. You can see this agreement very clearly in the second example.

Qui after a Preposition

You also use *qui* after a preposition when referring to people.

Let's look at some examples:

- *Elle pense à son fils. Son fils habite à Paris.* → *Le fils* **à qui** *elle pense habite à Paris.* (She is thinking about her son. Her son lives in Paris. → The son about whom she is thinking lives in Paris.)

- *Nous parlons de notre oncle. Notre oncle est très contrarié.* → *L'oncle* **de qui** *nous parlons est très contrarié.* (We are talking about our uncle. Our uncle is very upset. → The uncle about whom we're speaking is very upset.) (**Note:** For verbs that take *de*, the relative pronoun *dont* is also a possibility. We'll learn about *dont* in Unit 2.)

- *Les enfants voyagent avec une personne. La personne est leur belle-mère.* → *La personne* **avec qui** *les enfants voyagent est leur belle-mère.* (The children are traveling with a person. The person is their stepmother. → The person with whom the children are traveling is their stepmother.)

Some common prepositions that come up in this context are: *à, de, avec,* and *pour.*

You'll often see *qui* after the following verb + preposition combinations:

French verb + Preposition	English meaning
faire (quelque chose) pour	to do (something) for
jouer avec	to play with
parler avec	to talk with
parler de	to talk about
penser à	to think about
rêver de	to dream about
sortir avec	to go out with (to date)
travailler pour	to work for
travailler avec	to work with
vivre avec	to live with
voyager avec	to travel with

Summary of *Que* or *Qui*?

A handy way to remember whether to use *que* or *qui* as the relative pronoun is:

- ***que*** + subject + verb

- ***qui*** + verb

- preposition + ***qui*** when talking about <u>people</u>

Make sure to practice with the exercises at the end of this chapter.

The Pronoun *en*

The pronoun *en* is like a Swiss Army knife – one little word, multiple uses. You can use *en* when discussing quantities. You can also use *en* to replace phrases that are introduced by the preposition *de*. Each of these general uses include several possibilities, which makes *en* an extremely useful pronoun to know.

A bit of background before we look at specific examples. You will find *en* most helpful when the noun or phrase it's replacing has already come up in conversation. Otherwise, its use could create confusion, except in special cases where it forms part of a saying. (You'll find examples of these special sayings at the end of this section.)

So, if someone asks a question and you want to answer without repeating the subject or another noun in the question, you could use *en*. Another example could be where you're talking or writing and you've already raised an idea. If you want to make your next sentence shorter and less repetitive, you could use *en*.

Here's a sample conversation:
(Find the audio reference on page 4.)

Philippe: *As-tu des idées pour fêter l'anniversaire de mariage de maman et papa ?*
(Do you have any ideas for how to celebrate mom and dad's anniversary?)

Hélène: *Oui, j'**en** ai deux ou trois.*
(Yes, I have two or three. → *en* replaces "idées.")

Philippe: *Veux-tu m'**en** parler ?*
(Do you want to tell me about them? → *en* still refers to "idées.")

Hélène: *Non, je préfère les garder pour moi pour le moment. As-tu déjà acheté des cadeaux ?*
(No, I prefer to keep them to myself for now. Have you bought any presents yet?)

Philippe: *Oui, j'**en** ai déjà deux, mais il me faut de l'argent pour les autres.*
(Yes, I already have two, but I need money for the others – *en* replaces "cadeaux.")

Hélène: *Il t'**en** faut combien ?*
(How much do you need? → *en* replaces "argent.")

Philippe: *Je n'**en** sais rien. 200 euros ?*
(I have no idea. 200 euros? → *en* is part of a saying and does not replace a specific noun or phrase.)

This conversation would sound perfectly natural to a French-speaker even though *en* is used in several different ways throughout. Understanding the various uses of *en* will help you follow along.

Using *en* with Quantities

You can use *en* to replace a noun when the noun is modified by a suggestion of quantity. The quantity can be specific or undetermined. For example, you might be talking about "five cousins" or "some birthday cake" or "a lot of relatives." Let's look at how *en* might replace these nouns.

With a number:

Il a cinq cousins. (He has five cousins.) → *Il **en** a cinq.* (He has five (of them).)
Notice that only the noun is replaced. The number stays.

With partitive articles – *de, du, de la, des* (for things that can't be counted):

J'ai mangé du gâteau d'anniversaire. (I ate some birthday cake.) → *J'**en** ai mangé.* (I ate some (of it).)
Notice that the article <u>and</u> the noun are replaced.

With expressions of quantity:

Nous avons beaucoup de famille au Portugal. (We have a lot of relatives in Portugal.)
→ *Nous **en** avons beaucoup au Portugal.* (We have a lot (of them) in Portugal.)
Notice that only the noun is replaced. The expression of quantity stays.

Using *en* to Replace Phrases Introduced by *de*

A second category of uses for *en* is to replace phrases that start with the preposition *de*. In the French language, you use *de* after many verbs. It often translates to "about," such as with *parler de*, *rêver de*, or *penser de* (to express opinion). Some French verbs use *de* where the English equivalent does not require a preposition, such as *avoir besoin de* or *se souvenir de*.

Here are some examples of how *en* can replace a phrase that begins with *de* after a verb. (Find audio on page 5.)

Elle parle souvent de son enfance. (She talks about her childhood often.)
→ *Elle **en** parle souvent.* (She talks about it often.)

Les enfants rêvent de retourner à la plage. (The children dream about going back to the beach.)
→ *Les enfants **en** rêvent.* (The children dream about it.)

On a eu tous besoin de rire. (We all needed to laugh.)

🎧 → *On en a eu tous besoin.* (We all needed it.)

Mon père se souvient de son premier voyage en avion. (My father remembers his first plane trip.)

🎧 → *Mon père s'en souvient.* (My father remembers it.)

Common Expressions with *en*

Several French expressions use *en*. In these expressions, *en* is not replacing a word or phrase. It forms an integral part of the expression. So, there's no need for a prior reference. Your meaning will be loud and clear.

French expression	English meaning	Example
s'en aller	to leave	*Ils s'en vont.* (They are leaving.)
n'en pouvoir plus	to not be able to stand something any longer	*Elle n'en peut plus.* (She can't take it anymore.)
en avoir marre	to be fed up with something	*J'en ai marre.* (I've had enough.)
s'en faire (usually used in negative)	to worry, to care about	*Ne t'en fais pas.* (Don't worry.)
s'en vouloir (de)	to blame oneself (for)	*Elles s'en veulent.* (They blame themselves.)

Grammar Tips with *en*

To use *en* correctly, keep two things in mind.

En goes right before the conjugated verb. If there are any reflexive pronouns (*me, te, se, nous, vous*) that also go before the verb, those pronouns need to go before *en*. You can see this placement above with the examples: *Ils s'en vont* or *Ne t'en fais pas* or *Elles s'en veulent*.

Those examples also show the second point to remember. If the word before *en* ends in a vowel, you need to drop the vowel to form a contraction. This applies with the reflexive pronouns and with *ne*. You can see the *ne* + *en* contraction in the example: *Elle n'en peut plus.*

Make sure to practice with the exercises at the end of this chapter.

Demonstrative Articles

When you need to clarify that you are talking about one thing and not another, you use demonstrative articles. **This** book is better than **that** book. **These** exercises are more helpful than **those**.

French demonstrative adjectives follow the same general agreement rules as other adjectives. Masculine singular nouns require a masculine demonstrative adjective, and feminine singular nouns require a feminine one. For plural demonstrative articles, French does <u>not</u>, however, distinguish between masculine and feminine.

The French demonstrative adjectives are:

Ce: for masculine singular nouns.

Cet: for masculine singular nouns that begin with a vowel or a mute 'h.'

Cette: for feminine singular nouns.

Ces: for all plural nouns, whether masculine or feminine.

Here are some examples:

Ce cousin (this/that cousin)

Cet oncle (this/that uncle)

Cette tante (this/that aunt)

Ces cousins (these/those cousins)

Ces tantes (these/those aunts)

Did you notice there is only one French word for both this/that and these/those? Well, that's not the end of the story. To distinguish between near objects (this/these) and far objects (that/those), you can add *-ci* or *-là* at the end of the noun.

Here are some examples:

Ce cousin-ci (this cousin)

Ce cousin-là (that cousin)

Ces tantes-ci (these aunts)

Ces tantes-là (those aunts)

Vocabulary for Family Relationships

French term	English meaning
la mère	mother
le père	father
la sœur	sister
le frère	brother
les parents	parents (sp.), relatives (gen.)
la grand-mère	grandmother
le grand-père	grandfather
les grands-parents	grandparents
la tante	aunt
l'oncle	uncle
le cousin	cousin
la cousine	female cousin
la marraine	godmother
le parrain	godfather
la belle-mère	stepmother or mother-in-law
le beau-père	stepfather or father-in-law
le filleul	godson, godchild
la filleule	goddaughter

Vocabulary for Birthdays and Parties

l'anniversaire (m.)	birthday
le gâteau d'anniversaire	birthday cake
la bougie	candle
le cadeau	gift
la fête	party
le ballon	balloon
la carte de vœux	greeting card
les décorations (f.)	decorations
l'invité (m.)	guest
les félicitations (f.)	congratulations

EXERCISES III

1. **Complétez chaque phrase avec le pronom relatif <u>que</u> ou <u>qui</u>.**
   Complete each sentence with the relative pronoun <u>que</u> or <u>qui</u>.

   a. Les invités _____ sont venus à notre réveillon du Nouvel An étaient tous ravis.

   b. La tarte _____ mon cousin prépare est traditionnelle.

   c. Ma marraine n'aime pas la viande _____ est servie à Pâques.

   d. Le discours _____ ma mère a prononcé pour mon anniversaire était émouvant.

   e. Les amis avec _____ nous dînons le dimanche sont très proches de la famille.

   f. Le sapin de Noël _____ ma famille décore est très grand.

   g. Ma cousine porte une chemise _____ vient du Sénégal.

   h. Les bonbons _____ tu distribues chaque Halloween sont délicieux.

   i. Elle a écrit un livre _____ raconte l'histoire de sa famille.

   j. Mes parents construisent une maison _____ ils comptent léguer à mon frère.

   k. La grand-mère avec _____ je parle habite en Chine.

   l. Les enfants _____ figurent sur la photo sont mes neveux et nièces.

   m. La fête _____ vous célébrez est d'origine suédoise.

   n. Les chansons d'anniversaire _____ chante ma famille sont rigolotes.

   o. Les enfants pour _____ elle fait à manger sont ses filleuls.

2. **Transformez chaque phrase en remplaçant une partie avec le pronom « en. »**
   Transform each sentence by replacing one phrase with the pronoun "en."

   a. Mon cousin a amené des tartes.
   _____

   b. Son parrain organise un voyage par an.
   _____

   c. J'ai reçu plusieurs cartes de vœux hier.
   _____

   d. Nous nous souvenons de nôtre enfance.
   _____

   e. Ma belle-mère ne veut plus de commentaires.
   _____

   f. Ses oncles parlent toujours de football.
   _____

   g. Que pensez-vous de notre nouvelle maison ?
   _____

   h. Ma grand-mère possède trois voitures.
   _____

   i. Mon cousin rêve de se marier depuis longtemps.
   _____

   j. Au réveillon de Noël, nous buvons du champagne.
   _____

   k. Combien de frères et sœurs as-tu ?
   _____

   l. Elle offre de l'amour à tous ses prochains.
   _____

3. **Complétez chaque phrase avec l'adjectif démonstratif qui convient.**
   Complete each sentence with the appropriate demonstrative adjective.

   a. _____ enfant est très mignon. (This/That child is very cute.)

   b. _____ maison est ancienne. (This/That house is old.)

   c. _____ cousines sont gentilles. (These/Those cousins are nice.)

   d. _____ souvenirs sont difficiles. (These/Those memories are painful.)

   e. _____ dîner est copieux. (This/That dinner is heavy.)

   f. _____ fleurs sont magnifiques. (These/Those flowers are beautiful.)

4. **Rajoutez -ci ou -la pour préciser la signification exacte.**
   Add -ci or -la to specify the correct meaning.

   a. Cette fille _____ fête son anniversaire. (This girl is celebrating her birthday.)

   b. Ces années _____ sont passées vite. (Those years went by quickly.)

   c. Ce père _____ ramène toujours des gâteaux. (That father always brings cakes.)

   d. Ces jours _____ on aime se balader en forêt. (These days we like to walk in the forest.)

   e. Cette carte _____ vient de mon grand-père. (That card is from my grandfather.)

   f. Cet hôtel _____ a une grande salle de bal. (This hotel has a large ballroom.)

CHAPTER 4
Les Amis

While there is a common stereotype that French people are unfriendly, friends or *les amis* are a big part of French life. The French tend to remain close to their childhood friends for life. While forming friendships in adulthood may take time, these bonds typically last a lifetime.

C'est and *Ce* sont

If you want to introduce your friends or other acquaintances to people, the phrases *c'est* and *ce sont* will come in handy. For example:

- *C'est mon ami.* (This is my friend.)
- *Ce sont mes copains.* (Those are my pals.)

The phrases are constructed by combining the demonstrative *ce* and a conjugation of the verb *être*. The singular form, *c'est*, is the contraction of *ce + est* (*être* in the third person singular). The plural form is *ce + sont* (*être* in the third person plural).

The French use *c'est* and *ce sont* in several ways. The three primary uses are (1) for identifying people or things (as with the introductions above), (2) for emphasizing people or things, and (3) for describing people or things. Here are some examples of the three uses.

Identification

- *C'est un verre à vin.* (This is a wine glass.)
- *Ce sont des bars.* (These are bars.)

Emphasis

- *C'est mon verre qu'il a cassé.* (It's my glass that he broke. / My glass is the one he broke.)
- *Ce sont les bars qui font du bruit.* (It's the bars that make noise. / The bars are the ones making noise.)

Description

- *C'est offert/gratuit.* (It's complimentary / free.)
- *C'est parfait.* (It's perfect.)

For **identification** and **emphasis**, to choose between the singular and plural forms, you need to know how many people or things about whom you're talking. So, it's the subject after the verb that determines whether you use *c'est* (one person or thing) or *ce sont* (two or more persons or things). The base structure is as follows:

- *C'est* + singular noun
- *Ce sont* + plural noun

When using these phrases for **emphasis**, you add to the base structure a *que* or *qui* structure, which we learned in the last chapter.

- *C'est* + singular noun + *que* + subject + verb
- *C'est* + singular noun + *qui* + verb
- *Ce sont* + plural noun + *que* + subject + verb
- *Ce sont* + plural noun + *qui* + verb

Here are a few more examples to help you see that this **emphasis** structure is not as complex as the above diagrams might suggest.

- *C'est le gâteau qu'il a brûlé.* (The cake is what he burned.)
- *C'est Pauline qui a payé.* (It's Pauline who paid. / Pauline's the one who paid.)
- *Ce sont mes fourchettes qu'on a perdu.* (It's my forks that we've lost. / My forks are the ones we lost.)
- *Ce sont les serviettes qui sont sales.* (It's the napkins that are dirty.)

For **description**, it might sound awkward, but you always use the singular *c'est* followed by a singular adjective even if you're discussing multiple things.

Here are some examples:

- *C'est délicieux, ce plat.* (This dish is delicious.)
- *C'est cher, les restaurants.* (Restaurants are expensive.)

Make sure to practice with the exercises at the end of this chapter.

Direct and Indirect Complement Pronouns

French can be a flowery language, but the French are also very good at verbal table tennis where the proverbial ball is passed back and forth between speakers quickly. As you begin to have conversations in French, you will sometimes need to use shorter, punchier sentences.

Another set of pronouns that will help with this goal are the complement pronouns. These pronouns replace the objects in sentences. Direct complement pronouns replace the direct object, and – surprise! – indirect complement pronouns replace the indirect object.

Here are some English examples.

- **Direct**: I placed Pierre next to me. I placed **him** next to me.
- **Indirect**: I saved some dessert for Anaïs. I saved some dessert for **her**.

In English, we use the same set of pronouns for both direct and indirect complement pronouns: me, you, him, her, it, us, you (plural), them. In French, we need to look at the two categories separately.

Direct Complement Pronouns

Direct complement pronouns replace the noun that directly receives the action of the verb. In the example above, Pierre receives the action of the verb "to place."

The direct complement pronoun needs to match the noun it is replacing. Below is a table showing the direct complement pronoun that corresponds to each noun category in French.

Category	French direct complement pronoun
First person singular (*je*)	*me*
Second person singular (*tu*)	*te*
Third person singular, masculine (*il*)	*le*
Third person singular, feminine (*elle*)	*la*
First person plural (*nous*)	*nous*
Second person plural (*vous*)	*vous*
Third person plural, masculine or feminine	*les*

For the above example with Pierre, the French would be:

J'ai placé Pierre à côté de moi. Je l'ai placé à côté de moi.

A first point to note is that the direct complement pronouns that end in a vowel (*me, te, le, la*) drop their vowels in front of a verb that begins with a vowel. So, *le + ai* becomes *l'ai*.

Let's see what happens when I seat Marianne next to me.

J'ai placé Marianne à côté de moi. Je l'ai placée à côté de moi.

Hopefully, you noticed that one extra letter that tells us the person I placed is a woman. An –*e* has been added to *placé* because the object is feminine. The contraction *l'ai* in this sentence is formed by *la* + *ai*. So, a second point to note is that any past participle after the verb must agree with the object in both gender and number.

So, if I had seated Marianne and Chantal next to me, the sentence using direct complement pronouns would read: *Je les ai placées à côté de moi.*

To summarize, the three key things to remember about direct complement pronouns are:

1. Pick the direct complement pronoun that matches the noun you are replacing.

2. Contract direct complement pronouns *me, te, le, la* with verbs that begin with a vowel.

3. If there is a past participle after the verb, you must have agreement between the pronoun and the past participle.

Make sure to practice with the exercises at the end of this chapter.

Indirect Complement Pronouns

Indirect complement pronouns replace the noun that is indirectly affected by the action in the sentence. The indirect object often answers the question "for what / whom" or "to what / whom." We often introduce the indirect object with a preposition like "to" or "for." In fact, looking to see if you are replacing only a noun (direct object) or a noun + preposition (indirect object) is a handy rule of thumb for choosing between a direct complement pronoun and an indirect complement pronoun.

In the example above, with Anaïs, the direct object is "the dessert" – I saved it. For whom? For Anaïs. Anaïs is the indirect object.

As with the direct complement pronoun, the indirect complement pronoun needs to match the noun it is replacing. The table below shows the corresponding indirect complement pronoun for each noun category in French.

Category	French indirect complement pronoun
First person singular (*je*)	*me*
Second person singular (*tu*)	*te*
Third person singular, masculine or feminine	*lui*
First person plural (*nous*)	*nous*
Second person plural (*vous*)	*vous*
Third person plural, masculine or feminine	*leur*

For the above example with Anaïs, the French would be:

J'ai gardé du dessert pour Anaïs. Je lui ai gardé du dessert.

With indirect complement pronouns, a first point to note is that you do contract the *me* and *te* forms with verbs that begin with a vowel. The *lui* form does not, however, follow this rule. It remains intact as a separate word before verbs that begin with vowels.

Unlike with the direct complement pronouns, a past participle after the verb does not agree with an indirect complement pronoun. Recall that the indirect object is not receiving the action of the verb; so the participle does not relate directly to it. For the above example, you can see that "*gardé*" remains the same in both sentences.

The main thing to remember with indirect complement pronouns is to choose the correct form to match the noun you are replacing.

Vocabulary for Dinner with Friends

French term	English meaning
l'ami (m.)	friend (m.)
l'amie (f.)	friend (f.)
le copain	close friend (m.), also boyfriend
la copine	close friend (f.), also girlfriend
le / la pote	buddy, pal (informal)
ami(e) d'enfance	childhood friend
entre amis	among or with friends
le dîner	dinner
le repas	meal
l'entrée (f.)	starter (appetizer)
le plat principal	main course
le dessert	dessert
l'eau (f.)	water
le vin	wine
la bière	beer
le café	coffee
le thé	tea
l'apéritif (m.)	before-dinner drink
le digestif	digestive drink (after-dinner drink)
la carte	the menu
le menu	a set meal package (such as appetizer + main course)
commander	to order
cuisiner	to cook
manger	to eat
boire	to drink
dîner	to have dinner
le restaurant (slang: le resto)	restaurant
le bistrot	bistro: small, casual French restaurant
la brasserie	a type of casual restaurant often serving beer
le bar	bar

EXERCISES IV

1. **Complétez chaque phrase avec c'est ou ce sont.**
   Complete each sentence with c'est or ce sont.

   a. _____ des clients réguliers. (These are regular customers.)

   b. _____ un menu végétarien. (It's a vegetarian menu.)

   c. _____ des verres à eau. (These are water glasses.)

   d. _____ gras, les frites. (French fries are greasy.)

   e. _____ une table qu'il faut réserver. (This is a table that must be reserved.)

   f. _____ le chef du restaurant. (This is the chef of the restaurant.)

   g. _____ des plats copieux. (These are copious (big) dishes.)

   h. _____ cher, le homard. (Lobster is expensive.)

   i. _____ les desserts du jour. (These are the desserts of the day.)

   j. _____ un serveur qui est tombé. (It's a waiter who fell.)

2. **Traduisez chaque phrase en utilisant c'est ou ce sont.**
   Translate each sentence using c'est or ce sont. (If you do not know a word, look it up.)

   a. These are the drinks that we ordered.

   _____

   b. This is my kitchen.

   _____

   c. This is the restaurant that has a good atmosphere.

   _____

   d. These are the daily specials.

   _____

   e. This is the waiter who took our order.

   _____

3. **Complétez chaque phrase avec le pronom complément d'objet direct qui convient.**
   Complete each sentence with the correct direct complement pronoun.

   a. *Je prépare le dîner.* (I prepare dinner.)

      Je _____ prépare.

   b. *Nous avons invité nos amis.* (We invited our friends.)

      Nous _____ avons invités.

   c. *Justine apporte le dessert.* (Justine is bringing dessert.)

      Justine _____ apporte.

   d. *Vous emmenez mon mari et moi.* (You are taking my husband and me.)

      Vous _____ emmenez.

   e. *Mes copines décorent la salle.* (My (girl)friends are decorating the room.)

      Mes copines _____ décorent.

   f. *Il attend tes amis et toi à 19h.* (He expects you and your friends at 7 p.m.)

      Il _____ attend à 19h.

   g. *Les garçons mettent la table.* (The boys set the table.)

      Les garçons _____ mettent.

   h. *Tu as choisi cette brasserie.* (You chose this brasserie.)

      Tu _____ as choisie.

   i. *Le serveur remercie ma copine et moi.* (The waiter thanks my friend and me.)

      Le serveur _____ remercie.

   j. *Nous avons rangé les assiettes.* (We put away the plates.)

      Nous _____ avons rangées.

4. Complétez chaque phrase avec le pronom complément d'objet indirect qui convient.
Complete each sentence with the correct indirect complement pronoun.

a. *Ils expliquent les règles du jeu à leurs amis.* (They explain the rules of the game to their friends.)

   Ils _____ expliquent les règles du jeu.

b. *Nous racontons des blagues à toi.* (We tell you jokes.)

   Nous _____ racontons des blagues.

c. *Elle prodigue des conseils à sa copine.* (She gives her friend advice.)

   Elle _____ prodigue des conseils.

d. *Claire a écrit des cartes postales à ma cousine et moi.* (Claire sent postcards to my cousin and me.)

   Claire _____ a écrit des cartes postales.

e. *Mon père téléphone à son meilleur ami tous les jours.* (My father calls his best friend every day.)

   Mon père _____ téléphone tous les jours.

f. *Mes potes ont apporté du vin à moi.* (My buddies brought me some wine.)

   Mes potes _____ ont apporté du vin.

g. *Tu lis tes recettes à tes amis.* (You read your recipes to your friends.)

   Tu _____ lis tes recettes.

h. *Jessica parle souvent de ses rêves à mon ami et moi.*
   (Jessica often talks to my boyfriend and me about her dreams.)

   Jessica _____ parle souvent de ses rêves.

i. *Gilles emprunte un couteau à son ami.* (Gilles borrows a knife from his friend.)

   Gilles _____ emprunte un couteau.

j. *Philippe a raconté des histoires à tes enfants et à toi.*
   (Philippe told you and your children stories / lies.)

   Philippe _____ a raconté des histoires.

CHAPTER 5
Au Travail

In France, life at work is often very different from life outside of work. The relationships can be more impersonal and formal. While work colleagues can be friendly, in general they keep work relationships and friendship separate. Like everything, this social distance at work is changing, but in a French professional setting it is best to be formal until your French colleagues give explicit permission to be less formal. So, you will want to know a few social rules, including the proper way to address colleagues.

The Formal You (*Vous*)

The *vous* form of you can be used for the plural "you" when addressing multiple people. It can also be used to address only one person. When addressed to one person, the pronoun *vous* shows formality, respect, or politeness.

Vous can indicate distance in a relationship, such as with people who are not family or close friends. In more traditional families, sons-in-law and daughters-in-law will address their spouses' parents with *vous* no matter how long they have been married. Additionally, in some elite families, even spouses use *vous* to address each other as a mark of formality. The French have specific words for the use of *vous* – *le vouvoiement* – and the use of *tu* – *le tutoiement* – because these social practices remain important.

Many non-native French speakers use *vous* almost exclusively because they are afraid of causing offense by using the informal *tu* at the wrong time. It is a good idea to be mindful of when to use *tu* and when to use *vous*, and this section gives you some guidelines to choose the right form.

Workplace Etiquette

The French use *vous* in the workplace and other professional settings, such as when consulting with a doctor or interacting with a salesclerk in a shop. In the French workplace, respect for hierarchy can be extremely important, and employees typically address their superiors using *vous*, even when they have a very friendly relationship.

In younger, more modern workplaces, like start-ups, people are more likely to use *tu*. Like wearing jeans and a t-shirt instead of a suit, *tu* conveys the more casual office culture. Even then, with clients / customers or other external relationships, it is a good idea to use *vous* unless the client invites you to switch to *tu*.

Switching from *Vous* to *Tu*

In the workplace, it is a good idea to use *vous* initially to avoid seeming overly familiar or disrespectful. Here's some advice for how to know when it is safe to switch to *tu*:

- Most often, the other person will begin to use *tu* to address you and will expect you to follow along.

- If you do not pick up on this cue, the other person may ask or say explicitly *on peut se tutoyer*, which means "can we / we can address each other with the *tu* form." If phrased as a question, it is a good idea to say yes because insisting on *le vouvoiement* can create a chill in the relationship. If phrased as a statement, a good response is "*super*," meaning "great!"

- In some cases, you may notice that your peers are using *tu* between themselves, but they continue to use *vous* to address you. It may be that something about your position suggests to them that you are their superior or that distance should be maintained. You might ask one French colleague whom you trust whether *le tutoiement* is appropriate. If they think it's okay, you can then individually invite peers who are your age or younger to switch to *tu*

    – 🎧 *on peut se tutoyer?*

- Take care to show respect to people who are lower in the hierarchy, such as support or custodial staff, by addressing them with *vous*.

Using *Tu* from the Start

Outside the workplace, there are many situations where using *tu* is okay. For example, when addressing children, *tu* is expected. If you are invited into a close-friend group where everyone is around your age, *tu* is also generally expected. Some people may, in fact, pretend to feel slighted if you use *vous*. Some regions, such as the southwest (around Bordeaux and Toulouse) and the northwest coastal areas (Brittany), are also a bit more relaxed than Paris; you can observe how others interact to get some context clues. When in doubt, go with *vous* and switch to *tu* when it feels appropriate or when someone invites you to do so.

Make sure to practice with the exercises at the end of this chapter.

Tonic Pronouns

Tonic pronouns are a particularly French form of expression. Some French people find them annoying or overused, but they are still quite common and so important to know. So, what are they? When the French want to put emphasis on a personal pronoun (*je, tu, il, elle, nous, vous, ils, elles*) in a sentence, they will add a tonic pronoun. French tonic pronouns, also known as stressed pronouns or disjunctive pronouns, are often used for clarity or emphasis. They also are the correct personal pronoun form after prepositions.

The table below shows the French tonic pronouns.

French personal pronoun	French tonic pronoun	English meaning
Je	**moi**	me
Tu	**toi**	you
Il	**lui**	him
Elle	**elle**	her
On	**soi**	one
Nous	**nous**	us
Vous	**vous**	you
Ils	**eux**	them (m.)
Elles	**elles**	them (f.)

These tonic pronouns have three primary uses: for emphasis, after prepositions, and in comparisons. Let's look at each of these uses.

For Emphasis

When using tonic pronouns for emphasis, there are two main structures.

One emphasis structure uses *c'est* or *ce sont*, which we learned in Chapter 4. Here are some examples:

*C'est **moi** qui l'ai fait.* (I did it.)

*Ce sont **eux** qui doivent travailler plus.* (They are the ones who need to work harder.)

*C'est **toi** qu'il veut pour ce projet.* (You're the one he wants for this project.)

*Ce sont **nous** qu'on a virés.* (We're the ones who got fired.)

In these examples, we see two grammar points to keep in mind when using *c'est / ce sont* + tonic pronoun + *qui / que* construction.

First, when using *qui* after the tonic pronoun, the verb conjugation matches the tonic pronoun. In the first example, *ai* is the conjugation of avoir in the first-person singular to match *moi* (*je*). In the second example, *doivent* is the third-person plural conjugation of devoir to match *eux* (*ils*).

Second, when using *que* after the tonic pronoun, if there is a past participle it must agree with the tonic pronoun. In the fourth example, *virés* (the past participle of *virer* – to fire / let go) has an "–s" to agree with the plural *nous*.

The other emphasis structure using tonic pronouns is a little more controversial. Many French parents sometimes scold their children for using it. This use involves using both the tonic pronoun and the subject pronoun. The repetition adds emphasis. Let's explore some examples.

>   ***Moi**, je veux une augmentation de salaire.* (I want a (salary) raise.)
>
>   ***Elles**, elles ne viennent jamais aux réunions.* (They / Those ladies never come to meetings.)
>
>   ***Lui**, il sait comment obtenir ce qu'il veut.* (He knows how to get what he wants.)
>
>   *Vous me rendez la vie difficile, **vous** !* (You are making my life difficult.)

While it is most common for the tonic pronoun to come at the beginning of the sentence, it can also be added at the end. (Side note: It is the *moi, je* phrase that French parents often try to root out of their children's speech.) This structure is not common in English where voice inflection or pacing is the more common way to add emphasis to a personal pronoun. Some French speakers also prefer to rely on more subtle forms of emphasis. However, using the tonic pronoun / personal pronoun repetition, at least occasionally, will help your French sound more authentic.

After Prepositions

Using tonic pronouns after prepositions is not at all controversial and is, unquestionably, the proper grammatical form for referring to people after a pronoun. Here are some examples:

>   *Je souhaite collaborer **avec eux**.* (I want to collaborate / work with them.)
>
>   *Nous pensons **à elle** pour la promotion.* (We're thinking about her for the promotion.)
>
>   *Patron, nous avons organisé des visites **pour vous**.*
>   (Boss, we've organized some on-site visits for you.)

*On ne peut compter que **sur soi** dans ce bureau.* (One can count only on oneself in this office.)

*Henri demande toujours trop **de nous**.* (Henry always asks too much of us.)

Using tonic pronouns after prepositions is fairly straightforward. Just remember that tonic pronouns replace only personal pronouns, meaning that you use them only to refer to people, not things.

In Comparisons

For comparing people, tonic pronouns are a useful structure as they allow for clear, simple sentences. To use tonic pronouns for comparison, there are two basic structures:

Subject + **verb** + *plus / moins que* + **tonic pronoun**

For example: *Elle travaille plus que nous.* (She works more than we do.)
François gagne moins que toi. (François earns less than you do.)

Subject + être **conjugation** + *plus / moins* + **adjective** + *que* + **tonic pronoun**

For example: *Christine est plus compétente que lui.* (Christine is more competent than he is.)
Vous êtes moins râleur que moi. (You are less grouchy than I am.)

The one tricky thing with this structure is to make sure the verb conjugation – and, in the second structure, the adjective – matches the subject of the sentence, <u>not</u> the tonic pronoun.

Make sure to practice tonic pronouns with the exercises at the end of this chapter.

Including and Limiting

Some useful language for talking about groups or objects in the workplace – and elsewhere – are words that help you identify who or what is included or excluded from a description. You can use the following words and phrases to clarify whether someone or something is included or excluded from a particular context.

Including

The most common French words and phrases to express inclusion are *y compris* and *inclus*. They are used in slightly different ways.

Y compris is the equivalent of "including" in English, and you would use it in a separate clause. Below are a couple of examples:

Tous les membres de l'équipe, **y compris** *les nouveaux arrivants, doivent assister à la réunion.*
(All team members, including the newcomers, must attend the meeting.)

Les frais de voyage, **y compris** *les billets d'avion et l'hébergement, seront remboursés.*
(Travel expenses, including airfare and accommodation, will be reimbursed.)

Inclus is the equivalent of "included" in English, and you would use like an adjective incorporated into the main sentence. Below are a couple of examples:

Les frais de service sont **inclus** *dans la facture.*
(Service charges are included in the bill.)

Les cheffes d'entreprises sont **incluses** *dans les chiffres finaux.*
(The women business owners are included in the final figures.)

Because *inclus* is used as an adjective, it needs to agree with the gender and number of the subject of the sentence. Use *inclus* for masculine subjects, whether singular or plural. For feminine singular nouns, you will need to add "–e." For feminine plural nouns, you will need to add "–es."

Limiting

The most common French words and phrases to express exclusion are *sauf, excepté,* and **à part**. Again, each term is used in slightly different ways.

Sauf / Excepté

Both *sauf* and *excepté* translate to "except" in English. The grammatical use of the two words is also identical. Both are used as prepositions before a noun or a clause, such as in the following examples:

Les bureaux sont ouverts tous les jours **sauf / excepté** *le dimanche.*
(The offices are open every day, except Sunday.)

Tous les employés, **sauf / excepté** *ceux qui sont malades, doivent assister à la réunion.*
(All employees, except those who are ill, must attend the meeting.)

The terms are often used interchangeably for "except." The main difference between *sauf* and *excepté* is in their usage. *Sauf* is much more common in everyday use, especially spoken language and informal writing. *Excepté* is more formal; so, you are more likely to see and use it in formal writing or more formal contexts, such as a lecture or formal business setting.

À part

À part translates to "apart from" or "except for" in English. *À part* introduces a separate clause as you can see in the examples below:

À part quelques fautes de frappe, le rapport est complet et précis.
(Apart from a few typos, the report is complete and accurate.)

À part le service juridique, tous les départements ont surpassé leurs objectifs.
(Aside from the legal department, all departments exceeded their targets.)

The use of *a part* follows this basic structure:

à part + article / possessive / notion of quantity + noun.

Basic Work Vocabulary

French term	English meaning
le travail	work
le bureau	office
le patron / la patronne	boss
le collègue	colleague
le salaire	salary
la réunion	meeting
le poste	position
le congé (payé)	(paid) leave
le rapport	report
la tâche	task
le projet	project
le travail / le boulot (slang)	work, job
l'équipe (f.)	team
l'employé(e)	office worker
l'ouvrier / l'ouvrière	(blue collar) worker

EXERCISES V

1. **Pour chaque dessin, indiquez si l'utilisation de tu ou de vous sera plus appropriée.**
   For each sketch, indicate whether it is more appropriate to use tu or vous.

a.

b.

c.

d.

e.

f.

g.

h.

a. _____

b. _____

c. _____

d. _____

e. _____

f. _____

g. _____

h. _____

2. **Complétez chaque phrase avec le pronom tonique qui convient.**
   Complete each sentence with the correct French tonic pronoun.

   a. *Ils travaillent souvent pour _____ (us).*

   b. *Je veux discuter du projet avec _____ (you).*

   c. *Tu peux compter sur _____ (them, f.) pour le rapport annuel.*

   d. *Ce document vient de _____ (him).*

   e. *_____ (you), tu arrives toujours à l'heure.*

   f. *Elles sont parties à la réunion sans _____ (me).*

   g. *Mon collègue a fait livrer une lettre à _____ (them, m.) hier soir.*

   h. *_____ (us), nous sommes retournées au bureau.*

   i. *Le grand bureau est à _____ (you, formal).*

   j. *Nous devons collaborer avec _____ (her) sur ce dossier.*

3. **Traduisez chaque phrase en utilisant le pronom tonique qui convient.**
   Translate each sentence using the correct French tonic pronoun.
   (If you do not know a word, look it up.)

   a. My boss is more excited than I am.

   _____

   b. We travel less than they (f.) do.

   _____

   c. His colleague is less reliable than he is.

   _____

   d. Your assistant worked more than you (informal) did.

   _____

   e. Marc wrote more letters than we did.

   _____

   f. The new clients are more likable than they (m.) are.

   _____

4. **Complétez chaque phrase avec y compris ou inclus.**
   Complete each sentence with y compris or inclus.

   a. Les frais de livraison sont _____ dans le prix total.

   b. Tous les bureaux sont occupés, _____ ceux du sous-sol.

   c. Tous les membres de l'équipe, _____ la patronne, étaient présents à la réunion.

   d. Le résultat de ma recherche est _____ dans le rapport.

   e. Toutes les informations nécessaires sont _____ dans le document.

   f. Tous les clients, _____ les plus difficiles, ont apprécié la présentation.

5. **Complétez chaque phrase avec sauf, excepté ou à part.**
   Complete each sentence with sauf, excepté or à part.

   a. Les formations sont obligatoires _____ pour les stagiaires.

   b. _____ le projet en cours, nous n'avons pas d'autre travail.

   c. Tous les employés ont reçu un bonus _____ ceux qui ont démissionné.

   d. Les animaux sont formellement interdits au bureau _____ les chiens guides.

   e. Ils sont tous partis en vacances _____ Héloïse.

   f. Tu es disponible pour des réunions en semaine _____ quelques mercredis.

6. **Écoutez cette conversation entre Marie et Hugo et répondez aux questions de compréhension ci-dessous.**

   Listen to this conversation between Marie and Hugo and answer the listening comprehension questions below.

a. Où est allé Hugo cet été ?
   (Where did Hugo go this summer?)

   _____

b. Qu'a fait Marie pendant l'été ?
   (What did Marie do during the summer?)

   _____

c. Que vont faire Marie et Hugo la semaine prochaine ?
   (What are Marie and Hugo going to do next week?)

   _____

UNIT 2
School

Unit 2 focuses on life at school, including talking about a school schedule, talking about or participating during classes, and talking about school administrative matters, such as grades, teachers' conferences, and meetings with school administration. Whether you are a student, a teacher, a parent, or curious about French school life, this chapter has grammar and vocabulary that you will find useful.

CHAPTER 1
Talking about Time

In this chapter, we'll learn how to express the time and talk about a school schedule in French.

What's the time, please?

Let's begin with the basic vocabulary related to time in French. *Le temps* means "time" generally (it can also mean "the weather"), but it is not the word French speakers use for speaking about the time on a clock. Instead, they talk about the hour or *l'heure*. It's one example of how French is often a very precise language.

The Hours

To request the time of day, you ask *quelle heure est-il? - What hour is it?*

To indicate the time, the proper construction begins with *il est....* A common mistake that marks people as non-native French speakers is using *c'est* to indicate the time. Let's avoid that! The table below shows how to complete the phrase *il est...* to indicate the complete time in French.

Time	English phrasing	French phrasing
Top of the hour	It's one / two / three etc. o'clock	*Il est une heure.* *Il est deux / trois / etc. heure<u>s</u>.*
Exact time	It's five o'clock **sharp**.	*Il est cinq heures **pile**.*
Precise time up to 30 minutes	It's six twenty-four. (6:24)	*Il est six heures vingt-quatre.*
Precise time from 31-59	It's eight thirty-five. (8:35)	*Il est neuf heures **moins** vingt-cinq.* *
Quarter past	It's a quarter past nine. (9:15).	*Il est neuf heures **et quart**.*
Half past	It's half past ten. (10:30).	*Il est dix heures **et demie**.*
Quarter 'til	It's a quarter to one. (12:45).	*Il est une heure moins **le quart**.*
Noon	It's noon / midday. (12:00 p.m.)	*Il est **midi**.*
Midnight	It's midnight. (12:00 a.m.)	*Il est **minuit**.*

* While the French will continue to count the minutes past 30, it is more common to begin subtracting from the coming hour, especially for intervals of five minutes – *moins 25* translates to minus 25.

The 24-Hour Clock

The French most often use the 24-hour clock. That means that, instead of restarting the hour count at noon, the French continue counting the hours throughout the day. So, at 1:00 p.m. *il est treize heures* (13h), at 2:30 p.m. *il est quatorze trente*, at 3:45 p.m. *il est seize heures moins le quart*, and so on.

If you prefer to avoid the 24-hour clock until it becomes more familiar to you, you can use the 12-hour clock references. You will need, though, to specify the time of day with one of the following phrases: *du matin* (in the morning), *de l'après-midi* (in the afternoon), *du soir* (in the evening), *la nuit / du petit matin* (late night, very early morning). For example:

Il est quatre heures de l'après-midi.
(It's four o'clock in the afternoon.)

Il est dix heures du matin.
(It's 10:00 a.m.)

Nous dînons à huit heures du soir.
(We dine at 8:00 p.m.)

Je suis rentrée à une heure la nuit.
(I came in at one o'clock in the morning.)
→ *The time of day is noted here to emphasize the unusually late time.*

Time Sequences – Adverbs

To speak about time relative to now or about a sequence of events, we need to know adverbs related to time. Some common French adverbs of time for discussing schedule are shown here:

French term	English meaning
maintenant	now
avant	before
après	after
pendant	for (to express duration), during
ensuite	then, next
aujourd'hui	today
hier	yesterday
demain	tomorrow

When a noun follows the adverbs *avant*, *après*, and *pendant*, you must use an article even when one would not be used in English. For example: *avant le départ* (before departure), *après l'école* (after school), *pendant la soirée* (during the evening).

It is common for the adverbs *aujourd'hui*, *hier*, and *demain* to appear at the beginning of a sentence. For example:

Hier, je suis allée à l'école. (I went to school yesterday.)

Demain, nous avons un examen en maths. (We have a math exam tomorrow.)

Aujourd'hui, mon institutrice ne vient pas. (My teacher is not coming today.)

Expressing Duration

The French language has various ways of expressing duration, depending on when the event begins and how long it lasts. We saw above the adverb of time *pendant*, which means "for" or "during," and let's now look a bit closer at how to use *pendant* as compared to other ways of expressing the duration of an event. The other terms we will learn here are *depuis* and *pour*, which also (confusingly!) translate to "for" in English.

Using *Pendant*

Pendant can mean "for" or "during," based on the context in which you use it. When discussing the duration of a <u>past</u> event, we use *pendant* to express "for." Let's look at a few examples:

*Jean-Marie a étudié **pendant** deux heures.*
(Jean-Marie studied **for** two hours.)

*Le professeur a parlé **pendant** 30 minutes sans arrêt.*
(The teacher spoke **for** 30 minutes straight.)

*Les écoliers ont joué **pendant** toute la journée.*
(The school children played **for** the whole day.)

You may notice the examples all mention a bounded or identifiable period. When talking about a past event with a specified duration, *pendant* is the French word meaning "for."

Pendant means "during" when discussing an action that takes place in the midst of another event. For example, "Clarisse looks at her phone *during* class" or "Guillaume arrived *during* my presentation" or "Amélie will study *during* her vacation." Notice that "class," "presentation," and "her vacation" are events and not bounded time periods.

We can use *pendant* for past, present, or future situations when discussing these "intervening" actions (actions that happen during other actions). The French translations of the above examples are:

*Clarisse regarde son téléphone **pendant** les cours.*

*Guillaume est arrivé **pendant** ma présentation.*

*Amélie va étudier **pendant** ses vacances.*

Note that French includes the word *durant*, which also means "during." It has a slightly different meaning than *pendant*. Instead of suggesting an intervening event, *durant* implies one action lasts for the full duration of the other.

If, for example, we replaced *pendant* with *durant* in the first example above, it would mean that rude Clarisse looks at her phone for the entire time during her classes instead of once or occasionally. Similarly, poor Amélie would plan to study during her entire vacation rather than for part of the time. We could not use *durant* to talk about Guillaume's arrival unless he really took his time coming into the room – it's hard to imagine his arrival would last the full duration of my presentation.

Using *Depuis*

Depuis means "for" or "since," depending on the context. When discussing a time period that began in the past and is still ongoing, we use *depuis*. If we mention the starting point, *depuis* means "since." If, instead, we mention the time period, *depuis* means "for." Let's look at a few examples:

*Daphné enseigne la chimie **depuis** le mois de juin.*
(Daphné has been teaching chemistry **since** June.)
→ We mention when she started.

*Martin enseigne dans ce lycée **depuis** trois ans.*
(Martin has been teaching in this school **for** three years.)
→ We don't mention when he started, only how long it has been.

Using *Pour*

Pour means "for" when discussing the expected or intended duration of a period in the future. Again, some examples will help:

*Jérôme va **étudier** en Espagne **pour** une année.*
(Jérôme is going to study in Spain **for** a year.)

*Cécilia compte travailler **pour** trois mois.*
(Cécilia plans to work **for** three months.)

Aller and the Near Future

You have already learned to talk about the present (Workbook 1) and the simple past. Maybe you want to start looking forward. The verb *aller* is extremely helpful to talk about the near future or *futur proche*. *Aller* means "to go," and we can use it to talk about upcoming activities as with the English "to be going to."

To use *aller* to express the near future, the structure is:

subject + *aller* present tense conjugation + infinitive

Remember that *aller* is an irregular verb. The conjugation is shown here.

Pronoun	Present tense
Je	vais
Tu	vas
Il / elle	va
Nous	allons
Vous	allez
Ils / elles	vont

Let's look at a few examples for using *aller* for the *futur proche*:

*Nous **allons** apprendre le français.*
(We are going to learn French).

*Ils **vont étudier** après l'école.*
(They are going to study after school.)

*Je **vais** aller au collège l'année prochaine.*
(I'm going to go to middle school next year.)

Basic School Vocabulary

French term	English meaning
l'école (f.)	school
la rentrée (scolaire)	school opening, back to school
l'école maternelle (f.)	kindergarten
l'école primaire (f.)	primary school
le collège	middle school
le lycée	high school
l'université (f.)	university
le professeur / la professeure	teacher (generic) or professor (title)
l'enseignant (m) / l'enseignante (f.)	teacher (generic)
le maître (m.) / la maîtresse (f.)	kindergarten or primary teacher
l'écolier (m.) / l'écolière (f.)	grade school student
l'élève (m. / f.)	student
l'étudiant (m.) / l'étudiante (f.)	university student
le directeur (m.) / la directrice (f.)	principal (primary school)
le proviseur	principal (high school)
la classe	grade, class (meaning grouping of students)
le cours	class (meaning one class session or a subject matter, e.g., "math class")
la salle de classe / cours	classroom

EXERCISES I

1. **Pour chaque horloge, écrivez l'heure en français.**
   For each clock, write out the time in French.
   (If you use the 12-hour format, be sure to add the correct indication for time of day.)

a. 1:00 pm

d. (clock showing 6:00)

g. 6:15 pm

b. (clock showing ~1:55)

e. 5:10 am

h. 8:45 pm

c. 12:00 am

f. 12:00 PM

a. _____ e. _____
b. _____ f. _____
c. _____ g. _____
d. _____ h. _____

2. Écoutez le dialogue et remplissez les cases avec l'information manquante.
Listen to the dialogue and fill in the blanks with the missing information.

	lundi	mardi	mercredi	jeudi	vendredi
8:00 - 9:00	Anglais		Français	Politiques	Anglais
9:00 - 10:00			Chimie	Maths	Littérature
10:00 - 11:00	Histoire-géographie	Informatique	Économie	Art oratoire	Histoire-géographie
11:00 - 12:00	Maths	Politiques	Étude	Sports	
12:00 - 13:00	Déjeuner	Déjeuner	Déjeuner	Déjeuner	Déjeuner
13:00 - 14:00	Français	Sports	Anglais		Français
14:00 - 15:00	Arts-plastiques	Littérature	Histoire-géographie	Étude	Chimie
15:00 - 16:00	Chimie	Philosophie		Philosophie	Rattrapage

3. Complétez chaque phrase en utilisant pendant ou depuis.
Complete each sentence using pendant, or depuis as appropriate.

a. *Il étudie le français* _____ *trois ans.*
   (He has been studying French for three years.)

b. *Nous avons étudié l'histoire* _____ *une heure hier.*
   (We studied history for one hour yesterday.)

c. *Je vais travailler à la bibliothèque* _____ *trois heures cet après-midi.*
   (I am going to work at the library for three hours this afternoon.)

d. *Elles enseignent dans cette école* _____ *2019.*
   (They have been teaching at this school since 2019.)

e. *Ils vont faire une pause* _____ *quinze minutes.*
   (They are going to take a break for fifteen minutes.)

f. *J'ai pris des cours de musique* _____ *l'été dernier.*
   (I took music classes during the summer.)

4. Traduisez chaque phrase en utilisant le futur proche (aller + infinitif).
Translate each sentence using near future with **aller.** *(If you do not know a word, look it up.)*

a. I am going to study English in Australia.
   _____

b. The schools are going to close for the summer.
   _____

c. My teacher is going to write a children's book.
   _____

d. We are going to eat lunch after gym class.
   _____

e. You (sing., informal) are going to learn a lot in high school.
   _____

f. You (plural) are going to love the new library.
   _____

CHAPTER 2
In the Classroom

In this chapter, we'll learn vocabulary and grammar for talking about what happens in the classroom and for speaking up in class.

Obligation and Prohibition

What is school without rules? It is, therefore, useful to learn the most common expressions for explaining what is required and what must be avoided. The phrases *il faut* and *il ne faut pas* are French impersonal phrases for "one must" and "one must not." *Il faut* can also mean "it is necessary," and *il ne faut pas* can mean "it is prohibited / forbidden." (While these are the official translations, in everyday spoken French, when addressed directly to someone, the phrases mean "you have to" or "you should not / must not.")

In this chapter, we are going to study the simple structure for using these phrases. We will learn a more complex structure later in Unit 4 when we talk about the subjunctive.

The simple structure for *il faut* and *il ne faut pas* is to add the infinitive form of a verb. Here are two examples:

> *Il faut lever la main pour parler.* (One must raise one's hand to speak.)
>
> *Il ne faut pas bavarder pendant les cours.* (One must not talk during class.)

Knowing *il faut* and *il ne faut pas* will empower you to set or, at least, understand the rules.

Relative Pronouns: Dont and Où

As you may remember from Unit 1, Chapter 3, relative pronouns introduce a relative clause, meaning a phrase that adds detail about a noun in the sentence without needing to repeat the noun. In this section, you are going to learn two new relative pronouns: *dont* and *où*.

Dont

The French relative pronoun *dont* generally replaces phrases where the preposition *de* is followed by a noun. *Dont* can refer to both people and things. Because the preposition *de* is used in a variety of ways in French, the relative pronoun *dont* has a variety of meanings when translated to English.

To Replace Prepositional Phrases

You may remember that certain verbs require *de* before the object, such as *parler de* (to talk about), *avoir peur de* (to be afraid of), *se souvenir de* (to remember). In those cases, we can use *dont* to replace the phrase formed by *de* + noun to introduce a relative clause.

Some examples are helpful here:

- *Le professeur parle d'une histoire. L'histoire est drôle.*
  → *L'histoire dont le professeur parle est drôle.*

  The professor is speaking about a story. The story is funny.
  → The story **about which** the professor is speaking is funny.

- *J'ai peur d'un lycéen. Le lycéen est très grand.*
  → *Le lycéen dont j'ai peur est très grand.*

  I am afraid of a high school student. The high school student is very tall.
  → The high school student **that** I am afraid of is very tall.

- *Elles se souviennent d'une institutrice. L'institutrice a quitté l'école.*
  → *L'institutrice dont elles se souviennent a quitté l'école.*

  They remember a teacher from primary school. The teacher has left the school.
  → The teacher **whom** they remember has left the school.

(Usage note: You may remember that *en* is used to replace *de* + noun phrases. *En* is an adverbial pronoun, while *dont* is a relative pronoun. In other words, *en* works on its own and cannot introduce relative clauses, while *dont* typically works like *que* and *qui*, as discussed in Unit 1, Chapter 3.)

To Express Possession

Dont is also used to express possession. Because *de* is the French preposition that typically shows possession, this use of *dont* is consistent with replacing a prepositional phrase. The *de* in these cases is not, however, always obvious to English-speakers. Again, let's look at a few examples.

- *Nous avons un professeur. L'accent de notre professeur est belge.*
  → *Nous avons un professeur dont l'accent est belge.*

  We have a professor. The professor's accent is Belgian.
  → We have a professor **whose** accent is Belgian.

- *Charles préfère cette proviseure. Le mari **de** la proviseure joue au foot.*
  → *Charles préfère la proviseure **dont** le mari joue au foot.*

- Charles likes this principal. The principal's husband plays football (soccer).
  → Charles likes the principal **whose** husband plays soccer.

Où

You learned the word *où* in the Level 1 Workbook; it is the question word for "where." As a relative pronoun, *où* can mean "where," and it can also mean "when." *Où* is used to introduce a relative clause that adds details about place or time. Here are a couple of examples:

- *La salle de classe est équipée de micros. Nous étudions la rhétorique dans cette salle.*
  → *La salle de classe **où** nous étudions la rhétorique est équipée de micros.*

  The classroom has microphones. We study rhetoric in that classroom.
  → The classroom **where** we study rhetoric has microphones.

- *Un jour j'ai dit un gros mot en cours. Ce jour-là j'ai oublié de prendre le petit-déjeuner.*
  → *Le jour **où** j'ai oublié de prendre le petit-déjeuner, j'ai dit un gros mot en cours.*

  One day I said a curse word in class. That day, I forgot to eat breakfast.
  → The day (**that**) I forgot to eat breakfast, I said a curse word in class.

Indefinite Articles

We use indefinite articles to discuss non-specific people or things, such as "**a** school" or "**some** classes." The French indefinite articles are shown in the table below:

French indefinite article	When to use	Example	English meaning
Un	masculine, singular nouns	*un livre*	a book
Une	feminine, singular nouns	*une affiche*	a poster
Des	plural nouns (masculine and feminine)	*des bureaux (m)* *des tables (f)*	some desks some tables

A few special rules apply when using French indefinite articles. First, with expressions of quantity, the indefinite article is *de* instead of any of the above options. Similarly, in negative sentences, the indefinite article is also *de*. Finally, if an adjective is placed before the noun, once again, the indefinite article is *de*.

You'll find examples of these special cases below:

- *Nous avons beaucoup **de** devoirs cette semaine.* (We have a lot of homework this week.) (*Les devoirs* = homework. **Note,** however, we do not use *des* after *beaucoup*, an expression of quantity.)

- *Tu n'as pas **de** perspective sur le sujet.* (You don't have a view on the subject.) (**Note** that, in negative statements, *de* is the equivalent of "a.")

- *Ils ont **de** bonnes raisons de ne pas parler en cours.* They have good reasons for not speaking in class. (**Note** that, even though *raisons* is plural, because of the adjective *bonnes* <u>before</u> the noun, we use *de* instead of *des*. You can contrast this example with "*Ils ont **des** opinions douteuses.* They have questionable opinions." The adjective <u>after</u> the noun means you use one of the standard indefinite articles from the table above.)

School in France

The French education system is centralized under the authority of the Ministry of Education, which sets the national curriculum and academic standards. The Ministry of Education also sets the budgets, hires school personnel, and even organizes the school calendar (**calendrier scolaire**) for all public schools in France. In fact, the synchronized school holidays (**vacances scolaires**) cause major traffic jams during vacation transitions.

De la maternelle au lycée (From nursery to high school)

French school life is highly structured, both in terms of the curriculum and the daily interactions. Children's education is divided into four stages, with clear objectives for each stage. In **l'école maternelle** (ages 3-6), teachers focus on socialization and early childhood education, such as learning letters and numbers. During **l'école primaire** (ages 6-11), children learn basic reading and math, as well as beginning to learn what the French call **la culture générale**. Culture générale is considered fundamental knowledge about French history, culture, art, political institutions, and much more.

During **le collège** (a false cognate / *faux ami* that means middle school, ages 12-15), **les collégiens** study a broad curriculum that includes French language and literature, math, science, geography and history. Finally, in **le lycée** (ages 16-18), **les lycéens** select different paths of study that prepare them for the **baccalauréat** exam, a qualification that opens the doors to higher education, or alternatively that provide vocational training for future careers.

Les bons élèves (Good students)

In French schools, interactions between students and teachers tend to be formal. Signs of this formality include students' addressing teachers as "Monsieur" or "Madame" followed by their last name and using *le vouvoiement*. Teachers typically lecture rather than animate interactive discussions; although, when students reach high school, class participation and oral presentations become important evaluation methods. **Les bons élèves** listen attentively, take detailed notes, and respond to questions when the teacher calls on them.

Discipline is viewed as an essential element of education. Teachers typically address student misbehavior quickly and firmly. Punishments for violating school rules or policies may include verbal warnings or more formal disciplinary actions, such as suspension or, in particularly serious cases, expulsion.

The philosophy behind this formality and rigidity is that they create an environment in which students are better able to learn. Despite the discipline-oriented atmosphere, teachers do show concern for their students' development, including through parent-teacher conferences, student advising, and involvement with extra-curricular activities, such as student-led clubs or class trips.

 Listen to this description of a day in the life of a French high school student.

Classroom Vocabulary

French phrase	English meaning
le bureau	desk
la chaise	chair
le tableau	board (chalkboard)
le tableau blanc	whiteboard
l'affiche	poster
l'ordinateur (m.)	computer
le bavardage	unauthorized talking in class
faites attention, s'il vous plaît.	pay attention, please.
silence !	be quiet!
rangez vos affaires / vos téléphones.	put your things / phones away.
lever la main	to raise one's hand
poser une question	to ask a question
faire un exposé	to give a presentation
prendre des notes	to take notes
corriger les devoirs / les exercices	to correct homework / exercises
passer un examen	to take a test / exam
la colle (ex. : avoir une heure de colle)	detention (ex.: to receive one hour of detention)

✎ EXERCISES II

1. **Traduisez chaque phrase en français en utilisant il faut ou il ne faut pas.**
   Translate each sentence using il faut or il ne faut pas. (If you do not know a word, look it up.)

   a. It is prohibited to run in the halls.
   _____

   b. One must read all the books on the list.
   _____

   c. It is forbidden to yell at the teacher.
   _____

   d. It is necessary to know how to write well.
   _____

   e. One must not forget the instructions.
   _____

   f. One must respect different viewpoints.
   _____

2. **Complétez chaque phrase avec dont ou où le cas échéant.**
   Complete each sentence with either dont or où, as appropriate.

   a. Le livre _____ il a parlé est un classique de la littérature française.
   (The book he spoke about is a classic of French literature.)

   b. Le matin _____ nous avons étudié la Révolution française était fascinant.
   (The day we studied the French Revolution was fascinating.)

   c. Le collégien _____ j'ai parlé est très bavard.
   (The middle school student I spoke about is very chatty / talks a lot.)

   d. Le moment _____ le professeur entre, nous nous asseyons.
   (The moment the teacher enters we take our seats.)

e. *Les salles de cours _____ on trouve des tableaux blancs interactifs sont toutes occupées.*
(The classrooms where we would find a SMART board are all full.)

f. *Le sujet _____ nous débattons est complexe.*
(The subject we are debating is complex.)

g. *Le livre _____ elle a besoin pour ce cours est très cher.*
(The book that we need for this class is very expensive.)

h. *Le labo _____ vous avez fait vos expériences de chimie est bien équipé.*
(The lab where we did our chemistry experiments is well equipped.)

i. *L'élève _____ les idées sont les plus innovantes va recevoir un prix.*
(The student whose ideas are the most original will receive a prize.)

j. *Les jours _____ les profs font la grève, les écoles sont fermées.*
(The days when the teachers are on strike the schools are closed.)

3. Rédigez une phrase qui réunit les deux phrases en utilisant « dont » ou « où » le cas échéant.
Write one sentence that combines the two using either dont *or* où *as appropriate.*

a. *Jean assiste à ce lycée. Le débat va avoir lieu dans de lycée.*
(Jean goes to this high school. The debate will take place at this high school.)

_____

b. *Ces étudiants réussissent toujours au bac. Leurs parents sont des professeurs.*
(These students always pass the *baccalauréat* exam. Their parents are teachers.)

_____

c. *Ce cours de français est très demandé. Le prof du cours est un écrivain connu.*
(This French class is very popular. The professor for this class is a famous author.)

_____

d. *Il faut dire au revoir pour l'été. Ce moment n'est jamais facile.*
(We must say goodbye for the summer. This moment is never easy.)

_____

e. *Colin n'aime pas cette salle. Il fait très froid dans cette salle.*
(Colin does not like that room. It is very cold in that room.)

_____

f. *Béatrice a perdu un stylo. Elle a besoin de ce stylo pour son examen.*
(Beatrice lost a pen. She needs that pen for her exam.)

_____

4. **Complétez chaque phrase avec l'article indéfini qui convient – <u>un</u>, <u>une</u>, <u>des</u>, <u>de</u>.**
   Complete each sentence with the correct indefinite article – <u>un</u>, <u>une</u>, <u>des</u>, <u>de</u>.

   a. *Il y a _____ élèves qui parlent trop fort.*
   (There are (some) students who talk too loudly.)

   b. *Elle n'a pas trouvé _____ livre (m.) sur son bureau.*
   (She did not find a book on her desk.)

   c. *J'ai besoin d'emprunter _____ gomme (f.)*
   (I need to borrow an eraser.)

   d. *L'institutrice a mis _____ affiches éducatives sur les murs.*
   (The teacher put some educational posters on the walls.)

   e. *Nous avons _____ examen (m.) demain matin.*
   (We have an exam tomorrow morning.)

   f. *La proviseure espère _____ bons résultats pour le brevet.*
   (The principal hopes for good results on the middle school standardized test.)

   g. *Ils ont laissé _____ chaise libre à côté de la porte.*
   (They left an empty chair next to the door.)

   h. *On aborde beaucoup _____ sujets intéressants dans ce cours.*
   (We touch on many interesting topics in this class.)

   i. *L'école fournit _____ ordinateur (m.) pour chaque élève.*
   (The school provides a computer to each student.)

   j. *Clarisse n'a pas _____ feuille blanche (f.) à te prêter.*
   (Clarisse does not have a blank sheet of paper to lend to you.)

CHAPTER 3
Evaluations

This chapter focuses on grammar that is useful for evaluating a student's performance and progress. We'll look at how to talk about conversations, about changes in performance, and about reciprocal actions.

Reported Speech – Present

Whether you are a student trying to understand what a teacher is talking about or a teacher evaluating a student's class participation or behavior, you need to know how to report what they are saying. Reported speech refers to repeating what a person is saying or thinking without quoting directly.

Here's a quick example in English to show the difference:

Direct speech: Claire says: "This professor is very severe."

(Indirect) Reported speech: Claire says **that** this professor is very severe.

To talk about conversations indirectly in the present tense (*discours rapporté au présent*), the following rules will help for the two most basic situations: statements and simple inquiries.

For reporting **statements**, we use *que* to link the speaker to what they are saying. The above example in French would be: *Claire dit* **que** *ce professeur est très sévère.*

As we've already seen with *que*, in front of pronouns that begin with a vowel, the "e" in *que* is dropped to form a contraction (for example *qu'il, qu'elle*). For the pronoun *on*, you have a choice between (1) using the contraction *qu'on* and (2) adding "l" before the pronoun to form the phrase: *que l'on*. Both are grammatically correct, and there's no rule about which to use. The *l'* is a euphonic consonant, meaning it helps with pronunciation and musicality. Some prefer to avoid *qu'on* because to the ear it could be confused with a word that is an insult.

Let's look at a few more examples to clarify some additional points.

Martial dit : « je n'aime pas étudier l'histoire. » → Martial dit **qu'il** n'aime pas étudier l'histoire.

Martial says: "I don't like to study history." → Martial says that he doesn't like to study history.

Notre professeur dit : « vous allez beaucoup apprendre. »
→ *Notre professeur dit **que** nous allons beaucoup apprendre.*

Our teacher says: "You are going to learn a lot."
→ Our teacher says that we are going to learn a lot.

Point 1 – Pronoun and Conjugation Change: As with English, the pronoun may need to change in the reported speech to adapt to the context of the statement. When the pronoun changes, the verb conjugation also needs to change. This conjugation change is apparent in the second example above. (In the first example, *je* and *il* have the same form for the verb *aimer*.)

Les lycéens pensent : « Les cours sont trop difficiles et les devoirs prennent trop de temps. »
→ *Les lycéens pensent **que** les cours sont trop difficiles et **que** les devoirs prennent trop de temps.*

The high school students think: "the classes are too hard, and the homework takes up too much time." → The high school students think that the classes are too hard and (that) the homework takes up too much time.

Point 2 – Repeating que: When reporting a compound statement, meaning one that includes two statements, French requires that you repeat *que* before each reported statement. English-speakers often drop the second and any subsequent "that."

For reporting **simple inquiries**, we use *si* to link the speaker and what they are saying. Simple inquiry refers to a question that does not have a question word. Let's look at an example to help clarify.

L'institutrice demande à l'enfant : « Veux-tu des crayons colorés ? »
→ *L'institutrice demande à l'enfant **s'il** veut des crayons colorés.*

The teacher asks the child: "Do you want some crayons?" → *The teacher asks the child if he wants crayons.*

Les parents demandent au prof : « Allez-vous punir notre fils ? »
→ *Les parents demandent au prof **s'il** va punir leur fils.*

The parents ask the teacher: "Are you going to punish our son?" → The parents ask the teacher **if** he is going to punish their son.

You notice that the question is formed simply by reversing the subject and verb. It does not include words like *qui, que, quoi, comment*. You may also notice that in front of pronouns that begin with "i", the "i" in *si* is dropped to form a contraction. This rule does not apply with the pronouns *elle* or *elles*.

For the pronoun *on*, instead of dropping the "I," the French usually add "l'" before the pronoun to form the phrase: *si l'on*. This form avoids confusion with other words, such as the possessive *son*, and it flows better to the ear. While *si on* is grammatically correct, in spoken French *si l'on* is more common.

 Listen to the difference: *si on – si l'on*.

Progress Reports

An essential aspect of providing feedback is to describe a person's development over time. School evaluations include not only grades but also progress reports, which typically explain whether a student is doing better or worse in particular areas of interest.

More and Less

To talk about progress in French, the expressions *de plus en plus* and *de moins en moins* help describe gradual changes. *De plus en plus* translates to "more and more," and *de moins en moins* means either "less and less" or "fewer and fewer."

You can use the two expressions with nouns, verbs, adjectives, and adverbs to discuss changes. With verbs, adjectives, and adverbs, the phrases do not change. You simply insert them after the verb or before the adjective or adverb. Here are some examples:

Astrid étudie de plus en plus.	Astrid studies more and more.
Thomas bavarde de moins en moins.	Thomas chats less and less.
Michel est de plus en plus impliqué dans le cours.	Michel is more and more involved in class.
Emma est de moins en moins timide.	Emma is less and less shy.
Ghislaine écrit de plus en plus vite.	Ghislaine writes more and more quickly.
Charles interrompt de moins en moins souvent.	Charles interrupts less and less often.

For nouns, *de plus en plus* and *de moins en moins* are treated like expressions of quantity. As you learned in Chapter 2 of this Unit, in French, expressions of quantity are followed by the indefinite article *de*. Let's look at a couple of examples for this structure.

Christine a de plus en plus de confiance en soi.	Christine has more and more self-confidence.
Jérémie perd de moins en moins de livres.	Jérémie loses fewer and fewer books.

Frequency

Knowing expressions of frequency is also helpful for providing feedback and talking about progress. Here is a list of some common French expressions of frequency.

French term	English meaning
toujours	always
souvent	often
parfois	sometimes, occasionally
ne ... jamais	never
fréquemment	frequently
rarement	rarely
de temps en temps	sometimes, from time to time
régulièrement	regularly
quotidiennement	daily
tout le temps	all the time
tous les jours	every day
toutes les semaines	every week
tous les mois	every month
tous les ans	every year

A usage note with *ne... jamais*. The construction is similar to *ne... pas*. You therefore need to put *ne* before the verb rather than using *jamais* on its own. For example, *il n'arrive jamais en retard.* (He never arrives late.)

Pronominal Verbs

French pronominal verbs, or *les verbes pronominaux*, are verbs that we use with a reflexive pronoun (me, te, se, nous, vous, se). You have already learned about reflexive verbs, such as *se laver* (to wash oneself) or *s'habiller* (to dress oneself), which are one category of pronominal verbs.

In this section, we are going to study a category referred to as "reciprocal" verbs. They are called reciprocal because the action of the verb occurs between two or more people. In English, the phrase "each other" or "one another" appears with these types of verbs. In French, we use the reflexive pronoun to convey the reciprocity.

Let's look at a few examples for clarity:

Nous nous parlons souvent. We talk to each other often.

Les professeurs se comprennent sans dire un mot. (The teachers understand each other without saying a word.)

Les lycéens se connaissent depuis la maternelle. (The high school students have known each other since primary school.)

A list of common reciprocal verbs is below.

French reciprocal verb	English meaning
s'aimer	to love each other
s'appeler	to call each other
se battre	to fight with each other
se comprendre	to understand each other
se connaître	to know each other
se croiser	to cross paths, pass each other
se détester	to hate each other
se dire	to tell each other
se disputer	to argue with each other
s'écrire	to write to each other
s'embrasser	to kiss each other
s'entendre	to get along, agree with each other
se parler	to talk to each other
se promettre	to promise each other
se quitter	to leave each other, to part ways
se regarder	to look at each other
se rencontrer	to meet each other
se téléphoner	to call each other
se voir	to see each other

These verbs can be used as regular verbs where the action is performed in only one direction. For example, *il te voit à travers la fenêtre.* (He sees you through the window.)

When, however, the action is reciprocal, the pronominal form is required. The reflexive pronoun must match the subject. For example, *vous vous voyez à travers la fenêtre.* (You see each other through the window.)

EXERCISES III

1. **Complétez chaque phrase avec que ou si le cas échéant.**
   Complete each sentence with either que or si as appropriate.

   a. La mère de Faustine demande _____ sa fille rencontre des difficultés en sciences.
   (Faustine's mother asks whether her daughter is having problems in science.)

   b. Le directeur précise _____ les bulletins sont envoyés par courrier.
   (The school director explains that report cards are being sent by mail.)

   c. Arthur demande _____ il va avoir une réunion parents-professeurs la semaine prochaine.
   (Arthur asks if there is going to be a parent-teacher conference next week.)

   d. Madame Durand dit _____ Paul fait des progrès remarquables en anglais.
   (Mrs. Durand says that Paul is making excellent progress in English.)

   e. Le père de Stéphane affirme _____ son fils a besoin de soutien scolaire.
   (Stephane's father states that his son needs tutoring.)

   f. Le secrétariat dit _____ l'on peut consulter les notes en ligne.
   (The administrative office says that we / one can check grades online.)

   g. L'élève demande _____ il peut toujours améliorer sa note en biologie.
   (The student asks if he can still improve his grade in biology.)

   h. Le professeur confirme _____ tous les élèves ont réussi l'examen.
   (The teacher confirms that all students passed the test.)

   i. La proviseure annonce _____ elle organise une réunion d'information.
   (The principal announces that she is organizing an information meeting.)

   j. La professeure demande à Marie _____ elles peuvent discuter après le cours.
   (The teacher asks Marie if they can speak after class.)

2. **Transformez chaque citation en discours rapporté au présent.**
   Transform each direct quote into reported speech in the present tense.
   (If you do not know a word, look it up.)

a. *M. Flandrin demande aux élèves : « Avez-vous des questions ? »*
   (Mr. Flandrin asks: "Do you have any questions?")

   _____

b. *Les parents disent : « Nos enfants ne sont pas de mauvaises élèves. »*
   (The parents say: "Our children are not bad students.")

   _____

c. *La mère de Lucie demande : « Ma fille travaille-t-elle bien en classe ? »*
   (Lucie's mother asks: "Does my daughter work hard in class?")

   _____

d. *Le professeur demande aux collégiens : « Êtes-vous capable de faire attention durant le cours ? »*
   (The teacher asks the middle school students: "Are you able to pay attention during class?")

   _____

e. *Les lycéennes demandent : « Peut-on parler au conseiller d'orientation »*
   (The high school students ask: "May we speak with the guidance counselor?")

   _____

f. *Le proviseur dit : « Les profs doivent rendre les notes avant le 26 juin. »*
   (The principal says: "The teachers must submit grades by June 26.")

   _____

3. **Complétez chaque phrase avec de plus en plus ou de moins en moins le cas échéant.**
   Expand the following sentences by adding details using de plus en plus or de moins en moins.
   (Try to use each phrase an equal number of times.)

   a. *Les étudiants sont* (Students are…)
   _____

   b. *Les professeurs veulent* (Professors want…)
   _____

   c. *Les parents ont* (Parents have…)
   _____

   d. *Les enfants jouent* (Children play …)
   _____

   e. *Les salles de cours contiennent* (Classrooms contain …)
   _____

   f. *Les écoles enseignent* (Schools teach …)
   _____

4. **Traduisez chaque phrase en français en utilisant l'expression de fréquence qui convient.**
   Translate each sentence using the appropriate expression of frequency.
   (If you do not know a word, look it up.)

   a. Students are **often** unhappy with their grades.
   _____

   b. My French teacher **always** gives helpful feedback.
   _____

   c. Teachers **rarely** give grades without explanations.
   _____

   d. The math teacher corrects our homework **every day**.
   _____

e. The school organizes parent-teacher meetings **regularly**.
_____

f. The principal **never** criticizes teachers in public.
_____

g. Parents **frequently** request progress reports.
_____

h. Students receive report cards **every semester**.
_____

5. **Complétez chaque phrase avec le verbe pronominal qui convient.**
   Complete each sentence with the correct pronominal verb. (If you do not know a word, look it up.)

a. *Les élèves* _____ *avant l'examen.*
   (The students encourage each other before the exam.)

b. *Les parents d'élèves* _____ *à la sortie de l'école.*
   (The parents talk to each other at after-school pick-up.)

c. *Les professeurs* _____ *pour rendre leurs carnets de notes à temps.*
   (The teachers motivate each other to submit their grade books on time.)

d. *Sybille et moi* _____ *tous les soirs.*
   (Sybille and I call each other every night.)

e. *Toi et tes camarades de classe* _____ *pendant les cours difficiles.*
   (You and your classmates support each other during challenging courses.)

f. *Il ne faut pas* _____ *pour des bêtises.*
   (You should not argue with each other over trifles.)

g. *M. Martin et Mme André* _____ *dans le couloir.*
   (Mr. Martin and Mrs. Andre pass each other in the hallway.)

h. *Les proviseurs de l'académie* _____ *pour une année réussie.*
   (The district principals congratulate each other on a successful year.)

6. Écoutez chaque phrase et indiquez s'il s'agit d'une citation ou du discours rapporté.
Listen to each sentence and indicate whether it is a direct quote or reported speech.

_____
_____
_____
_____
_____
_____
_____
_____
_____

UNIT 3
Work

Unit 3 focuses on looking for a job, interviewing for a position, and ending a work relationship. In France, workers at all levels have employment agreements. So, this section includes some vocabulary related to contracts and negotiation.

CHAPTER 1
Job Searches and Offers

In this chapter, we'll explore grammar and vocabulary that could be useful in searching for a job and evaluating job offers.

The Passive Voice and Ways to Avoid It

The passive voice refers to the grammatical form where the person or thing that receives the action of the verb becomes the subject rather than the object of the sentence. The doer of the action appears at the end of the sentence or, in some cases, disappears altogether. The passive voice can be useful when you want to emphasize the action or the recipient of the action, when you want deliberately to be vague about who is responsible, when announcing a general truth, or when the doer of the action (the agent) is unimportant or unknown.

Here is an example of an active voice sentence and its passive voice equivalent in English.

>**Active**: Job seekers request more information about the job openings.

>**Passive**: More information about the job openings is requested by job seekers.

To **form the passive voice in French**, there are four main points to remember. First, you use the auxiliary verb *être* **(to be)** + ***participe passé*** **(past participle)** of the main verb. Second, the conjugation of *être* must agree with the subject of the sentence (not with the agent). Third, because we are using *être*, the past participle must also agree with the subject of the sentence. Finally, to introduce the agent, we use the word *par* (by). If you need to use a pronoun after *par*, use one of the tonic pronouns (*moi, toi, lui, elle, nous, vous, eux, elles*) which we studied in Unit 1.

In French, the passive construction above would become: *Plus d'information concernant les postes vacants est sollicitée par les demandeurs d'emploi.*

While the passive voice has its appropriate uses, in many cases avoiding the passive voice adds clarity. Additionally, in spoken French, active constructions often sound more natural and informal than the passive voice. Let's look at a few alternatives you can use to avoid the passive voice even if the agent is unknown.

Reflexive verbs provide a great alternative to the passive voice. As a reminder, reflexive verbs are one category of "pronominal verbs" where we use a reflexive pronoun with the verb to express the direction of the action. While it might seem odd that reflexive pronouns can refer to things other than people, we can indeed use them with concepts or things.

Have a look at these examples:

> **Passive voice :** *Les offres d'emploi <u>sont postées</u> sur le site de l'entreprise.*
> Job offers are posted on the company website.

> **Reflexive verb :** *Les offres d'emploi <u>se postent</u> sur le site de l'entreprise.*
> Job offers post on the company website.
> (Note that English does not have a good equivalent for this construction.)

> **Passive voice :** *Les compétences techniques <u>sont acquises</u> par la formation.*
> Technical skills are acquired through training.

> **Reflexive verb :** *Les compétences techniques <u>s'acquièrent</u> par la formation.*
> Technical skills develop through training.
> (Note again that English doesn't have a good equivalent for this construction, and we may need to use a different verb to translate while keeping the active voice.)

To use this technique, conjugate the main verb – associated with the past participle – as a reflexive verb by adding *se* before the verb and using the conjugated form that agrees with the subject of the sentence.

Another alternative to the passive voice is the **pronoun *on***. You can use this impersonal third-person pronoun as the agent, especially where the true agent is unknown. Here are some examples:

> **Passive Voice :** *Les candidatures <u>sont examinées</u> dans l'ordre de leur réception.*
> Applications are examined in the order they are received.

> **Impersonal *on* :** *<u>On examine</u> les candidatures dans l'ordre de leur réception.*
> One examines / They examine applications in the order they are received.

> **Passive voice :** *Les entretiens d'embauche <u>sont programmés</u> chaque jeudi.*
> Job interviews are scheduled every Thursday.

Impersonal *on* : <u>On programme</u> les entretiens d'embauche chaque jeudi.
They schedule job interviews every Thursday.

To use this technique, conjugate the main verb – associated with the past participle – in the third-person singular to agree with *on* as the subject of the sentence.

Adverbs ending in *-ment*

Adverbs in French commonly end with *-ment*, which is similar to the -ly ending English speakers use for adverbs. Creating adverbs by using an adjective + *-ment* follows a few important rules.

In most cases, form the adverb by adding *-ment* to the <u>feminine</u>, singular form of the adjective. For example:

sûr → *sûre* → *sûrement* (surely)

heureux → *heureuse* → *heureusement* (happily)

fou → *folle* → *follement* (madly, insanely)

In a few cases, you will need to add an accent to the adverb that does not appear in the adjective. An *accent aigu* (acute accent) is sometimes added to the *e* before *-ment* so that the syllable is pronounced when speaking. Without the accent, the pronunciation could be ambiguous, and the adverb would not sound as fluid. Here are a few examples of this particularity:

profond → *profonde* → *profondément* (deeply, profoundly)

confus → *confuse* → *confusément* (vaguely, confusedly)

For adjectives that end with a vowel, form the adverb by adding *-ment* to the <u>masculine</u>, singular form of the adjective. For example:

absolu → *absolument* (absolutely)

vrai → *vraiment* (really, truly)

For adjectives that end in -ant or -ent, spelling changes are necessary to avoid having two nasal sounds back-to-back. Recall French is a lyrical language and adding -ment after -ant or -ent would sound too harsh. To avoid this cacophony, change -ant to -am and -ent to em before you add -ment. This spelling change allows the adverb to flow more smoothly off the tongue. Have a look at two examples that show this spelling change:

> constant → constamment (constantly)
>
> évident → évidemment (evidently)

One exception to this rule is the adjective *lent* (slow). Instead of adjusting the spelling, you use the feminine form so that the adverb is *lentement* (slowly).

Making Comparisons

Comparison involves evaluating two things and determining whether one thing has more, less, or the same of some quality as the other. In English, many common adjectives and adverbs have comparative forms, such as smart – smarter or fast – faster, to express the superior comparison.

For many other adjectives and adverbs, the superior comparison requires using "more ... than." For example, "more competent than" or "more quickly than." The inferior comparison requires using "less...than" or "not as...as" and the equivalent comparison "as...as." Examples of these are "less intelligent than" or "not as smart as" or for equivalent "as fast as."

Whether comparing nouns or actions, the French use the same three basic structures: *plus ... que* ("more ... than"), *moins ... que* ("less ... than"), and *aussi ... que* ("as _ as"). What goes in the blank in these phrases is the adjective or the adverb that is the basis for the comparison.

When comparing using adjectives, the adjective form must agree with the subject in terms of gender and number. The following examples show the necessary agreement:

> *Ce candidat est moins préparé que les autres.*
> This candidate is less prepared than the others.
>
> *Elle est aussi qualifiée que vous pour le poste.*
> She is as qualified as you (are) for the position.
>
> *Nous sommes plus expérimentés qu'eux dans ce domaine.*
> We are more experienced than they are in this field.

For adverbs, comparison is simpler as the adverb form does not change. Here are a few examples.

Elle progresse dans sa carrière plus rapidement que ses collègues.
She is progressing in her career more rapidly than her colleagues.

Il postule aux offres d'emploi moins fréquemment que ses amis.
He applies to job offers less frequently than his friends.

Vous préparez vos lettres de motivations aussi minutieusement que nous.
You prepare your cover letters as thoroughly as we do.

Job Search Vocabulary

French term	English meaning
un emploi	a job
le poste	position
une annonce	job advertisement
le CV (curriculum vitae)	resume
la lettre de motivation	cover letter
une compétence	a skill
le stage	internship
le candidat / la candidate	applicant, candidate
la candidature	application
le recruteur	recruiter
l'entretien (d'embauche)	(job) interview
une offre d'emploi	job offer
l'embauche (f.)	(the act of) hiring
un contrat de travail	employment contract
le salaire	salary
la promotion	promotion

EXERCISES I

1. **Transformez chaque phrase de la voix active à la voix passive.**
   Transform each sentence from active voice to passive voice.

   a. *Le recruteur évalue les candidats.*
      (The recruiter evaluates the candidates.)
      _____

   b. *Je mets à jour mon CV.*
      (I update my resume.)
      _____

   c. *L'entreprise reçoit de nombreuses candidatures chaque jour.*
      (The company receives numerous applications every day.)
      _____

   d. *Noah passe des entretiens (m.) d'embauche.*
      (Noah has job interviews.)
      _____

   e. *Le cabinet concède nos prétentions (f.) salariales.*
      (The firm accepts our salary demands.)
      _____

   f. *Mon frère recherche un poste d'informaticien.*
      (My brother is looking for a position in IT.)
      _____

2. **Réécrivez chaque phrase en utilisant une alternative à la voix passive.**
   Rewrite each sentence using an alternative to the passive voice.

   a. *Le salaire est versé à la fin du mois.* (Salary is paid at the end of the month.)
   _____

   b. *Les compétences sont perdues sans usage constant.* (Skills are lost without constant use.)
   _____

   c. *Une offre d'emploi est présentée après les entretiens réussis.*
      (A job offer is made after successful interviews.)
   _____

   d. *Aucune embauche n'est formalisée pendant une grève.* (No hire is formalized during a strike.)
   _____

   e. *Sa demande d'augmentation est acceptée.* (His request for a raise is accepted.)
   _____

   f. *Ma recherche de travail est arrêtée pour l'été.* (My job search is stopped for the summer.)
   _____

3. **Convertissez chaque adjective en adverbe.**
   Convert each adjective into an adverb.

   a. *sérieux* (serious) _____

   b. *claire* (clear) _____

   c. *prudent* (prudent) _____

   d. *résolu* (resolved) _____

   e. *patient* (patient) _____

   f. *précis* (precise) _____

   g. *agréable* (pleasant) _____

   h. *attentif* (attentive) _____

4. Complétez chaque phrase avec le comparatif qui convient.
Complete each sentence with the appropriate comparison form.
(If you do not know a word, look it up.)

a. *Mon patron est* _____ *le tien.*
 (My boss is less understanding than yours is.)

b. *Notre recherche avance* _____ *l'on souhaite.*
 (Our job search is advancing more slowly than we want.)

c. *Ce stage est* _____ *mon précédent.*
 (This internship is as educational as my previous one.)

d. *Ce poste exige quelqu'un* _____ *lui.*
 (That position requires someone more experienced than he is.)

e. *Cette entreprise répond* _____ *les autres.*
 (This company responds less quickly than the others.)

f. *Ses qualifications sont* _____ *celles de l'autre candidat.*
 (Her qualifications are more impressive than those of the other candidate.)

g. *On peut se former* _____ *ici qu'ailleurs.*
 (One can be trained more completely here than elsewhere.)

h. *Cette nouvelle offre est* _____ *l'ancienne.*
 (This new offer is as attractive as the old one.)

CHAPTER 2
Job Interviews

In this chapter, you'll learn how to ask and answer questions during a job interview, including how to talk about your past experiences. We'll also revisit some positive and negative emotions that could come up in this context.

Perfect tense with *avoir*

This section focuses on the perfect tense using the auxiliary verb *avoir*. We introduced this tense in the final chapter (Unit 5, Section 4) of the first book in this series and we looked at the auxiliary verb *être* in Unit 1, Chapter 1 of this book.

Let's review once more: the French perfect tense or *passé composé* is used to talk about past actions. This one tense is used for both the English-language simple past tense ("I loved it") and the English-language present perfect tense ("I have loved you for a while.")

The perfect tense is called the *passé composé* in French because it is composed of three parts: *subject/pronoun + conjugated <u>auxiliary</u> verb + past participle of the <u>main</u> verb*.

We saw that when *être* is the auxiliary verb, the past participle of the main verb must agree with the subject. With more basic constructions using *avoir* as the auxiliary verb, we don't need to worry about changing the past participle.

But, when your sentences start to become more complex, you may need to pay attention to past participle agreements. In cases where the direct object comes before the verb, agreement is necessary.

The direct object can come before the verb in a couple of circumstances. First, when you use a relative pronoun (which we studied in Unit 1, Chapter 3), the relative clause often precedes the verb. Let's look at a few examples:

On a perdu le CV que j'ai envoyé. (They lost the resume that I sent.)

In this example, the agreement is not obvious because *CV* is masculine singular.

Le recruteur semble aimer les réponses que j'ai données.
(The recruiter seems to like the answers that I gave.)

In this example, the agreement is apparent because *réponses* is feminine plural.

The second structure that could place the direct object before the verb is when you use a direct object pronoun: *me, te, le, la, nous, vous, les*. When one of these pronouns replaces the object in a sentence, it always goes before the verb. Even though the verb is *avoir*, the past participle needs to agree with the object – not the subject. Here are two examples to demonstrate this agreement.

> *Ma position était précaire. On l'a terminée.*
> (My job was precarious. They ended it.)

> In this example, the participle agrees with *l'*, which replaces the feminine singular *position*.

> *Les entretiens sont essentiels. Nous les avons réussis.*
> (Interviews are essential. We did well in them.)

> In this example, the participle agrees with *les*, which replaces the masculine plural *entretiens*.

The perfect tense is extremely helpful in interviews as it allows you to talk about your education and past experience. Knowing when to create object-past participle agreement will allow you to use more complex sentences and avoid needless repetition.

Open-Ended Questions

Open-ended (or open) questions are questions that allow the person responding to supply whatever information they believe is relevant rather than limiting their responses to a closed set of options. Open-ended questions are the kinds of questions that draw out more detailed descriptions or information. They are well-suited for job interviews because they allow the recruiter to understand the candidates' experience as well as how they think and express themselves. They also allow candidates to obtain information about their potential employer.

The main French question words for asking open questions are in the chart below along with their English equivalents:

French question word	English meaning
qui	who
que / quoi	what
où	where
quand	when
pourquoi	why
comment	how

With these words you can form questions that elicit more information than closed questions – meaning those that can be answered simply with yes or no. Below are a few examples of each type of question:

Closed question : *Avez-vous déjà de l'expérience dans un cabinet d'avocat ?*

Do you have experience in a law firm?

Open question : *Où avez-vous déjà travaillé ?*

Where have you worked previously?

Closed question : *Est-il parti hier ?*

Did he leave yesterday?

Open question : *Quand est-il parti ?*

When did he leave?

Closed question : *A-t-elle démissionné à cause de son superviseur ?*

Did she quit because of her supervisor?

Open question : *Pourquoi a-t-elle démissionné ?*

Why did she quit?

Talking About Rules

In Unit 2, Chapter 2, we talked about rules at school using the *il faut / il ne faut pas* + infinitive construction. Well, the workplace also has rules that you might learn about or ask about during a job interview. So, let's learn some new vocabulary for talking about what is permitted, what is required, and what is prohibited.

In French, the verb **devoir** expresses obligation. It translates loosely as "to be required / obligated to" or "must" in the context of the sentence. Unlike *il faut*, which is impersonal and always conjugated in the third person, *devoir* is a personal verb. It can be used with the full range of personal pronouns and nouns and is conjugated to agree with the subject. *Devoir* is an irregular verb. You'll find its conjugation in the table below:

Je	*dois*
Tu	*dois*
Il / Elle / On	*doit*
Nous	*devons*
Vous	*devez*
Ils / Elles	*doivent*

The structure for using *devoir* is: **subject/pronoun + conjugated *devoir* + infinitive**. The following sentences provide helpful examples.

> *Tous les candidats <u>doivent fournir</u> des références professionnelles.*
> (All candidates must provide professional references.)

> *Vous <u>devez démontrer</u> votre capacité à travailler en équipe.*
> (You must show your ability to work as part of a team.)

Another possibility for expressing obligation is the phrase *être* **obligé**. This phrase literally translates as "to be obliged." The verb **être** is conjugated to match the subject / pronoun. As you might expect when you see the verb **être**, the adjective *obligé* must agree with the subject as to number and gender. One additional point with this structure is that the word *de* is added before the infinitive of the verb that is the obligation. The full structure is: **subject/pronoun + conjugated *être* + *obligé* (modified as necessary to agree with the subject) + *de* + infinitive**

While that might seem like a lot of moving parts, you have already learned how to conjugate *être* and how to create agreement between adjectives / participles to the subject. With practice, you'll be able to put all that knowledge together. Here are a couple of examples to reassure you that the structure looks more complicated than it is.

Nous <u>sommes obligés</u> d'évaluer vos compétences techniques lors de cet entretien.
(We're obligated to / We must evaluate your technical skills during this interview.)

Cette candidate <u>est obligée de</u> retirer sa candidature.
(That candidate has to withdraw her application.)

Great workplaces are not only about obligations. They also provide employees with opportunities to learn new skills and try new things. Knowing how to express permission will be useful in those situations. The verb ***pouvoir*** means "to be able to." It can be used to talk about capabilities (as in "You can") or to express permission (as in "You are allowed to"). For both meanings, the structure for using *pouvoir* is: **subject/pronoun + conjugated *pouvoir* + infinitive**.

You can also use *pouvoir* in the negative to express either an incapacity ("You are not able to") or a prohibition ("You are not allowed to"). Again, for both meanings the structure is: **subject/pronoun + *ne* + conjugated *pouvoir* + *pas* + infinitive**.

Pouvoir is an irregular verb. You'll find its conjugation in the table below:

Je	peux
Tu	peux
il / elle / on	peut
Nous	pouvons
Vous	pouvez
ils / elles	peuvent

Let's look at examples of permission and prohibition using *pouvoir*:

Vous pouvez poser des questions à la fin de l'entretien.
(You may ask questions at the end of the interview.)

Les candidats ne peuvent pas utiliser leurs téléphones portables pendant l'épreuve technique.
(Candidates cannot use their mobile phones during the technical test.)

EXERCISES II

1. **Traduisez chaque phrase en veillant à respecter la conjugaison et l'accord.**
   Translate each sentence, paying close attention to conjugation and agreement.

   a. The cover letter that she sent has typos (*fautes de frappe*).

   b. The candidates we interviewed are not qualified.

   c. The resume that I looked at is impressive.

   d. Did he accept the offer? He accepted it yesterday.

   e. The work I did in that position is relevant.

   f. Why did he leave his last job? He left (it) because of the low salary.

   g. The questions that they asked are very personal.

   h. The recruiter sent you flowers. I put them on your desk.

2. **Lisez chaque réponse et écrivez la question ouverte la plus probable d'avoir été posée.**
   Read each response and write the open-ended question most likely to have been asked.

   a. *Je gère le stress en prenant des pauses régulières.*
      (I manage stress by taking regular breaks.)

b. *Je veux ce poste parce qu'il correspond parfaitement à mes compétences.*
(I want this position because it corresponds perfectly to my skills.)

_____

c. *Je sais que votre entreprise est un leader dans ce secteur.*
(I know that your company is a leader in this sector.)

_____

d. *J'ai travaillé en Chine pendant deux ans après l'université.*
(I worked in China for two years after university.)

_____

e. *J'aimerais commencer le 1er septembre.*
(I would like to start on September 1st.)

_____

3. **Traduisez chaque phrase en français en utilisant <u>devoir</u>, <u>être obligé de</u>, ou <u>pouvoir</u>.**
   Translate each sentence using <u>devoir</u>, <u>être obligé de</u>, or <u>pouvoir</u>.

   a. We must check your references.

   _____

   b. Job seekers may obtain free advice.

   _____

   c. The company is required to disclose salaries.

   _____

   d. Interviewers may not ask questions about your health.

   _____

   e. You must arrive on time for your interview.

   _____

4. Écoutez la conversation suivante entre une recruteuse, Marie-France, et un candidat, Sébastien durant un entretien d'embauche. Lisez d'abord le texte pendant que vous l'écoutez. Ensuite, lisez à voix haute durant votre deuxième écoute.
Listen to the following conversation between a recruiter, Marie-France, and a candidate, Sébastien, during a job interview. First, read the script as you listen to it, and then try to read it aloud as you listen a second time.

[English translation is on the next page]

Marie-France : Bonjour Sébastien. Je vous en prie, installez-vous.

Sébastien : Bonjour madame. Merci.

Marie-France : Vous postulez pour devenir gouvernant à l'Hôtel de France, c'est bien ça ?

Sébastien : Oui, c'est ça.

Marie-France : Quelle est votre expérience dans le domaine ?

Sébastien : J'ai fait une formation en alternance à l'Hôtel de la Ville. J'ai suivi des cours d'hôtellerie et j'ai été homme de chambre puis chef d'étage dans un hôtel cinq étoiles pendant deux ans.

Marie-France : Qu'est-ce qui vous motive à devenir gouvernant ?

Sébastien : Le rythme me convient. D'ailleurs, j'aime la propreté et surtout le rangement.

Marie-France : Selon vous, quelles sont les qualités d'un bon gouvernant ?

Sébastien : Il faut être organisé et rigoureux pour repérer les oublis et les manquements.

Marie-France : Dernière question. Quelles sont vos prétentions salariales ?

Sébastien : J'aimerais un salaire mensuel de 1 950 € net.

Marie-France : Étant donné votre expérience, c'est envisageable.

Marie-France:	Hello Sébastien. Please take a seat.
Sébastien:	Hello, madam. Thank you.
Marie-France:	You are here because you applied for the housekeeping supervisor job at the Hotel de France, correct?
Sébastien:	Yes, that's correct.
Marie-France:	Do you have experience in this field?
Sébastien:	I had a work/study position at the Hotel de la Ville. I have taken hospitality courses, and I worked as a housekeeper and a floor supervisor in a five-star hotel.
Marie-France:	Why do you want to become a housekeeping supervisor?
Sébastien:	I like the work hours. Additionally, I like cleanliness and order.
Marie-France:	In your view, what are the qualities of a good housekeeping supervisor?
Sébastien:	You need to be organized and meticulous to spot errors and oversights.
Marie-France:	One last question. What are your salary expectations?
Sébastien:	I would like a net salary of €1,950 a month.
Marie-France:	Given your experience, that salary is possible.

CHAPTER 3
You're Fired! I Quit!

In this chapter, you'll learn how to part ways with an employer. Whether it is your decision, a mutual decision, or the employer's decision, knowing how to negotiate, compromise, and disagree will be necessary to burn only those bridges that you're ready to set on fire.

Complex Negation

Negation refers to denying an assertion or contradicting a statement. You learned the basic structure for negation in French – *ne ... pas* – in our first workbook. *Ne ... pas* is useful for expressing what is "not." If, however, you want to express negatives such as never, nothing, nobody, or no longer, you'll want to know the following structures.

Basic negation: *ne ... pas*

As a quick review – which will also help with understanding how the other structures work – to express "not" in French, you place *ne* before the conjugated verb and *pas* after it. In the *passé composé* (perfect tense) *pas* is placed before the past participle. Remember that *ne* becomes *n'* before verbs that begin with a vowel or an "h" that is not aspirated. Finally, you learned in Unit 2, Chapter 2 that after *ne ... pas*, indefinite and partitive articles disappear, and we use only *de* before the noun. Let's look at a few examples.

>*Je n'aime pas mon patron.* (I don't like my boss.)
>
>*Les ouvriers n'ont pas accepté notre offre.* (The workers did not accept our offer.)
>
>*Nous ne trouvons pas de solutions.* (We are not coming up with solutions.)

Never: *ne ... jamais*

Ne ... jamais is used to express "never." This structure works in an almost identical way to *ne ... pas*. One point of difference is that, in spoken French, it is common to hear *jamais* used at the start of a sentence for emphasis. When *jamais* starts the sentence, you still place *ne* before the verb, but no additional word after the verb. Here are some examples.

>*Christian ne voit jamais les qualités de ses employés.*
>(Christian never sees his employee's good qualities.)

Jamais elles n'ont volé de fournitures du bureau.
(They never stole any office supplies.)

Nothing: *ne ... rien*

Ne ... rien is used to express "nothing" or "not ... anything." This structure also works in an almost identical way to *ne ... pas*. Similarly to the *ne ... jamais* structure, in spoken French, it is common to hear *rien* used at the start of a sentence. Unlike with *jamais*, this alteration is often necessary because *rien* is the subject of the sentence. You'll find a few examples for using *ne ... rien* below.

Vous ne savez rien sur les rumeurs de licenciements ?
(You don't know anything about the rumors of layoffs?)

Charlène n'a rien fait pour mériter une convocation.
(Charlène did not do anything to warrant a formal notice.)

Rien ne peut me faire changer d'avis.
(Nothing can make me change my mind.)

No longer / not any-more / no more: *ne ... plus*

Ne ... plus is used to express "no longer" / "not ... anymore" or "no more" / "not ... any more." It can be used to say that a period of time has ended (no longer / not ... any more) or to talk about reaching the limit of a quantity (no more / not ... any more.) This structure also works in an almost identical way to *ne ... pas*.

The following examples should clarify the different ways you can use *ne ... plus*.

Je ne travaille plus ici.
(I no longer work here. / I do not work here anymore.)

Elles ne veulent plus d'heures supplémentaires.
(They do not want any more overtime (hours).)

Nous ne pouvons plus accepter ces conditions de travail.
(We can no longer accept these working conditions.)

Les patrons n'ont plus de patience pour les grévistes.
(The bosses no longer have patience / have no more patience for the striking workers.)

Je n'en peux plus.
(I can't take (it) anymore.) – This is a very common expression of exasperation in French!

Please note that when *ne ... plus* is used as a negative phrase, the 's' on *plus* is silent. When *plus* is used to express the word "more," the 's' is pronounced.

 Listen to the difference between these two sentences.

Nous ne voulons plus de drame. (We do not want any more drama.)

Nous voulons plus de congés payés. (We want more vacation days.)

Nobody / no one: *ne ... personne*

Ne ... personne is used to express "nobody" or "no one" or "not ... anyone." Like *ne ... pas*, the structure typically works by surrounding the conjugated verb. Like *ne ... jamais* and *ne ... rien*, the order is often altered so that *personne* begins the sentence. As with *rien*, this alteration is often necessary because *personne* is the subject of the sentence. Let's examine a few sentences to see how *ne ... personne* works.

L'entreprise n'a trouvé personne pour reprendre ce poste.
(The company did not find anyone to take over this position.)

Tu n'as personne à qui parler au bureau ?
(You have nobody you can talk to at the office?)

Personne ne souhaite démissionner. Ils veulent tous rester.
(Nobody wants to quit. They all want to stay.) – Note that *personne* is the subject of the first sentence.

Personne n'est dupe.
(Nobody is fooled.) – This is a common French expression to call someone's bluff or point out that they are failing to convince others.

Only: *ne ...que*

Ne ... que is used to express "only." This negative structure often trips up English speakers because the English equivalent does not contain an apparent negative. It can be helpful to think of *ne ... que* as expressing the idea of "nothing but." *Ne ... que* works in an almost identical way to *ne ... pas* with one key difference. After *ne ... que*, the original indefinite and partitive articles remain. Recall that after *ne ... pas*, these articles become *de*.

Here are a few examples that show how to use *ne ... que*.

Arnaud ne travaille que le matin.
(Arnaud only works in the morning.)

Le contrat proposé ne dure que trois mois.
(The proposed contract lasts only for three months.)

On n'a reçu que des chocolats en guise de bonus de fin de l'année.
(We received only chocolates as our end-of-year bonus.) – Note the indefinite article *des* stays the same rather than become *de*.

Les employés ne disent que du bien de la nouvelle convention collective.
(The employees have only good things to say about the new collective bargaining agreement.)

Many other negation structures exist in French, but this review of the most common should put you in good shape for when a simple "no" will not do.

Opposition and Concession

Cultural differences in communication are often visible in ways that people disagree. While some may find French people very open with their disagreement, they actually value nuance and reason in a spirited debate. It is common to hear the phrase *je ne suis pas d'accord* (I disagree). The phrase **être** *d'accord* means to be in agreement or to agree.

French includes many phrases for maintaining a respectful tone and being more diplomatic in presenting opposing views. Some of these softeners are in the table below.

French phrase	English meaning
cependant, toutefois	however
néanmoins	nevertheless
pourtant	yet, though
au contraire	to the contrary
en revanche	on the other hand
malgré	despite
en même temps	at the same time

Direct confrontation does occur. So, be prepared to say *je ne suis pas d'accord* or *je ne peux pas accepter cela* (I cannot accept that). If you do reach agreement, you can use the phrase *je suis (entièrement) d'accord* (I agree (completely)) or one of three simple words – *d'accord* (agreed), *soit* (OK – note: the "t" is pronounced), or *entendu* (understood).

When negotiating work contracts, knowing bigger numbers can be useful.

French term	Number
cent	100
mille	1,000
deux mille cinq cents (Note: It would be highly unusual to express this as *vingt-cinq cents*.)	2,500
dix mille (Note: *Mille* is invariable. In other words, do not add an "s.")	10,000
trente-trois mille	33,000
un million	1,000,000
un milliard	1,000,000,000

EXERCISES III

1. **Complétez chaque phrase avec le mot de négation qui convient.**
   Complete each sentence with the appropriate negation word.

   a. *Nous ne disposons _____ deux semaines pour répondre.*
   (We have only two weeks to respond.)

   b. *Vous ne perdez _____ en acceptant cette offre.*
   (You lose nothing by accepting this offer.)

   c. *_____ ne trouve la rémunération suffisante pour ces responsabilités.*
   (Nobody finds the compensation sufficient for these job requirements.)

   d. *L'entreprise n'acceptera _____ ces conditions.*
   (The company will never accept these conditions.)

   e. *Les syndicats ne veulent _____ d'embauches en contrat à durée déterminée.*
   (The unions don't want any more hires using short-term contracts.)

   f. *Les stagiaires n'ont _____ la possibilité de travailler en alternance.*
   (Interns no longer have the possibility to do work/study arrangements.)

   g. *Ils n'ont envoyé _____ pour négocier à leur place.*
   (They didn't send anyone to negotiate on their behalf.)

   h. *_____ ne pourrait remplacer les congés payés supprimés.*
   (Nothing can replace the canceled vacation days.)

2. Écoutez la négociation suivante entre un chef d'entreprise, Lucas, et un représentant du personnel, Chantal. Remplissez les blancs avec les mots manquants.
Listen to the negotiation between a business owner, Lucas, and an employee representative, Chantal. Fill in the blanks with the missing words.

[English translation is below]

Lucas : Bonjour, Chantal. Je comprends que vous avez des demandes pour améliorer les conditions de travail.

Chantal : Oui, Lucas. Les employés ne souhaitent plus d'heures supplémentaires, car ils sont très fatigués.

Lucas : Je comprends. _____, il est important pour l'entreprise de respecter les délais de production.

Chantal : Nous comprenons cela aussi. Mais, _____ cela, nous demandons des pauses plus longues pour nous reposer.

Lucas : _____, je vais voir ce que je peux faire pour allonger les pauses. Peut-être quinze minutes supplémentaires ?

Chantal : Merci, Lucas. Nous apprécions cet effort. De plus, il serait bien d'améliorer la ventilation sur le site.

Lucas : C'est un investissement conséquent, mais _____ nous devons assurer un environnement sain.

Chantal : Nous savons que cela implique des coûts. _____, les employés se sentiront mieux et seront plus productifs.

Lucas : Merci, Chantal. Nous allons travailler ensemble pour améliorer cela.

112 Unit 3 | *French Made Easy Level 2*

Lucas: Hello, Chantal. I understand that you have requests to improve working conditions.

Chantal: Yes, Lucas. The employees do not want any more overtime hours, as they are very tired.

Lucas: I understand. However, it is important for the company to meet our production deadlines.

Chantal: We understand that, too. But, despite that, we're asking for longer breaks so that we can rest.

Lucas: Okay, I will see what I can do to extend the breaks. Maybe an additional fifteen minutes?

Chantal: Thank you, Lucas. We appreciate this effort. Moreover, it would be good to improve ventilation on the site.

Lucas: That is a substantial investment; but at the same time, we need to ensure a healthy environment.

Chantal: We know it involves costs, but on the other hand, the employees will feel better and be more productive.

Lucas: Thank you, Chantal. We will work together to improve this.

UNIT 4
Hobbies

Unit 4 is about *les loisirs*, which loosely translates to hobbies and leisure interests. It's about the things people do for fun and distraction. We'll look at four big categories: movies, sports, arts and crafts, and charity and volunteer work.

CHAPTER 1
Movies

Le cinéma is a very popular leisure pursuit for French people. They see movies and discuss them with friends and critique them during dinners and repeat the lines of popular films as collective inside jokes. French popular culture (remember *la culture générale* from Unit 2, Chapter 2) includes general knowledge of many films. Seeing cult classic comedies like *La Grande Vadrouille*, *Les Visiteurs*, *Un Dîner de Con*, or *Les Bronzés* will help you better understand some conversations as references to them come up frequently. Classic dramas, such as *Les 400 Coups* or *La Guerre des Boutons*, can give insight into the French psyche and nostalgia. The French movie industry is quite active and well-regarded internationally. So, you can hopefully find at least one great French film you'll love.

Verbs for Talking about Sequences

Once you see that film that you love, you'll probably want to tell people about it. Being able to describe a sequence of events, including the various phases of actions or events, is essential to summarizing movie scenes and plots. Two verb phrases are very useful for talking about sequences: *venir de* (to have just ...) and *être en train de* (to be in the midst of ...).

***Venir de* + infinitive** is used to indicate that an action has just occurred. This verb phrase emphasizes that an action occurred very recently. You can use it to convey immediacy as compared to older actions. When using this construction, the verb *venir* is typically conjugated in the present even though talking about the recent past. (This statement does not apply for more complex past tense constructions that you'll learn in more advanced French levels.) Let's look at a few examples of *venir de*.

> *Je viens de voir un film époustouflant.*
> (I just saw an amazing movie.)
>
> *Nous venons de découvrir cet acteur.*
> (We just discovered this actor.)
>
> *Elles viennent de se rendre compte que l'homme les espionne.*
> (They just realized that the man is spying on them.)

***Être en train de* + infinitive** is used to indicate that an action is currently happening. It's similar to saying "to be in the process of" or "to be in the midst of." The French use *être en train de* to emphasize that the action is ongoing; it gives the action more of a sense of continuity than simple present or gerund forms. This construction is straightforward; you simply conjugate the verb *être*.

Here are some examples of how to use **être** en train de.

> *Est-ce qu'on veut vraiment voir ce film ? Jean est en train d'acheter les billets.*
> (Do we really want to see this film? Jean in the process of buying tickets.)
>
> *Veux-tu boire un verre ? Je suis en train de partir.*
> (Do you want to have a drink? I'm about to leave.)

Expressing an Opinion

Another tool for talking about movies is the ability to express an opinion. Two verb phrases are useful for sharing your views: *penser que* (to think that) and *trouver que* (to find that).

You can use the verb phrase *penser que* to express thoughts or impressions about something. To use *penser que*, conjugate the verb *penser* and use *que* as a relative pronoun to introduce the phrase that contains your opinion. These examples show how to use *penser que*:

> *Je **pense que** ce réalisateur a beaucoup de talent.* (I think that this director has a lot of talent.)
>
> *Nous **pensons que** le film était trop long.* (We think that the movie was too long.)

The verb phrase *trouver que* is also used to express opinions and is interchangeable with *penser que*. The grammatical structure is the same: conjugate the verb *trouver* and use *que* as a relative pronoun to introduce the phrase that contains your opinion. These examples show how to use *trouver que*:

*Il **trouve que** ce film est très émouvant.*
(He finds that this movie is very moving.)

*Elles **trouvent que** les effets spéciaux paraissent artificiels.*
(They find that the special effects look fake.)

Please note that, in the example sentences, the phrases with *penser que* and *trouver que* are affirmative statements. If the phrases were negative (*Je ne pense / trouve pas que ...*) or interrogative (*Penses-tu / Trouves-tu que ...?*), the relative clause would require the subjunctive tense, which you will learn in Chapter 4 of this unit.

Below are some adjectives that you'll find helpful for expressing general opinions or describing movies:

French adjective	English meaning
formidable	fantastic
intéressant/ (e)	interesting
incroyable	incredible
étonnant(e)	amazing
magnifique	magnificent
ennuyeux/ennuyeuse	boring
décevant(e)	disappointing
médiocre	mediocre
pas terrible	not great
horrible	horrible
captivant(e)	captivating
émouvant(e)	moving
hilarant(e)	hilarious
surprenant(e)	surprising
époustouflant(e)	stunning

 EXERCISES I

1. **Complétez chaque phrase avec la conjugaison de « venir de » ou « être en train de » qui convient.**
   Complete each sentence with the appropriate conjugation of "venir de" or "être en train de".

   a. Les enfants _____ entrer dans un monde magique.
   (The children just entered a magical world.)

   b. Le héros _____ sauver la ville d'une invasion extraterrestre.
   (The hero is saving the city from an alien invasion.)

   c. Les rebelles _____ préparer une attaque.
   (The rebels are preparing an attack.)

   d. Les enquêteurs _____ trouver un indice crucial.
   (The investigators just found an important clue.)

   e. Le pirate _____ naviguer vers une île inconnue.
   (The pirate is sailing toward an unknown island.)

   f. Le détective _____ rencontrer un témoin clé.
   (The detective just met with a key witness.)

   g. Le cambrioleur _____ voler les diamants.
   (The burglar just stole the diamonds.)

   h. Les aventuriers _____ découvrir un trésor caché.
   (The adventurers are in the midst of discovering a hidden treasure.)

   i. Le scientifique _____ avertir le président.
   (The scientist just warned the president.)

   j. La princesse _____ se libérer de la tour.
   (The princess is freeing herself from the tower.)

2. **Utilisez le résumé du film ci-dessous comme model pour rédiger un résumé pour un film que vous avez vu.**

   Use the below movie summary as a model to write a summary for a film that you've seen.

Le fabuleux destin d'Amélie Poulain	*Amélie Poulain, une jeune femme parisienne, **est en train de** découvrir la joie de créer du bonheur pour les autres. Elle **vient de** trouver une boîte secrète et décide de la rendre à son propriétaire. **Je trouve que** ce film est touchant et visuellement captivant.* Amélie Poulain, a young Parisian woman, is discovering the joy of creating happiness for others. She has just found a secret box and decides to return it to its owner. I find that this film is touching and visually captivating.
Votre choix de film (Your choice of film)	_____ _____ _____ _____ _____ _____ _____ _____ _____ _____

CHAPTER 2
Sports

In France, sports are a popular leisure activity and topic of conversation. Fans might meet at a local pub to cheer on the national team, Les Bleus. Alternatively, *licenciés* (people enrolled in an amateur sports association) might suit up to cycle a stage of the Tour de France. Whether watching or playing, the French engage passionately in their favorite sports.

Common sports include some that are globally popular, such as *le foot* (short for *football*, meaning soccer), *le rugby*, *le tennis*, and *le basket* (short for *basketball*). Other sports popular in France include *le handball*, *l'escrime* (fencing), and *le judo*, in which French teams and athletes often excel in international competitions. Many sports have organized and well-funded amateur programs that allow children to begin learning at an early age and help identify potential future champions.

To discuss sports, a few grammatical structures will be helpful: being able to express before, after, and during timing sequences; prepositions related to time; and superlatives.

Earlier, Later, at the Same Time

We've already looked at some adverbs and verbs for talking about sequences of events. Let's learn a few more structures to specify the timing and order of different actions. Talking about time relations in French requires specific structures for anterior (earlier), posterior (later), and simultaneous (at the same time) events.

Anterior (Earlier)

For talking about actions that happen earlier than other actions in a sequence, you can use the phrase **avant de** + **infinitif** (before + the verb in the infinitive form). This structure is equivalent to the English "before + the gerund (-ing) form." For example:

> **Avant de jouer** au tennis, elle s'échauffe.
> (**Before playing** tennis, she warms up.)

Please note that *avant que* is a second grammatical structure for discussing anterior actions. It requires the subjunctive form of the verb, which we'll look at in Chapter 4. So let's leave it aside for now.

Posterior (Later)

For talking about actions that happen later than other actions in a sequence, there are two possibilities.

The first structure is **après** + **infinitif du verbe auxiliaire** + **participe passé du verbe principal** (after + auxiliary verb infinitive + past participle of main verb). The auxiliary verb refers to *avoir* or *être*; the choice depends on the main verb, as we saw in Unit 1. This structure is equivalent to the English "after + the gerund (-ing) form."

Here are examples with *avoir* and *être*:

> **Après avoir couru** un marathon, il se repose.
> (**After running** a marathon, he rests.)

> **Après être tombée** de la poutre, elle se relève.
> (**After falling** from the balance beam, she gets back up.)

The second structure for talking about posterior actions is **après que** + **indicatif** (after + verb in the indicative mood). The indicative refers to using the verb to express factual information. The most common verb tenses for our purposes are the present or the perfect tense. Let's look at examples using each of these tenses.

> **Après qu'elle marque** un but, l'équipe le fête en dansant.
> (**After she scores** a goal, the team celebrates by dancing.)

> **Après qu'il a commencé** à pleuvoir, nous avons interrompu le match.
> (**After it started** to rain, we suspended the match.)

Simultaneous (at the Same Time)

For talking about actions that happen at the same time, you, again, have two options.

The first possibility is **en + *participe présent*** (while + gerund (-ing) form). Here's an example:

> ***En nageant***, *elle pense à sa respiration.*
> (**While swimming**, she thinks about her breathing.)

The second possibility for simultaneous actions is ***pendant que* + *indicatif*** (while + verb in the indicative mood). Let's look at a present tense example:

> ***Pendant qu'elle*** *s'entraîne, on observe sa foulée.*
> (**While she trains**, we monitor her stride.)

Prepositions of Time

Prepositions of time link nouns, pronouns, and phrases to indicate specific times, durations, or periods for when something happens. These prepositions are essential in providing context and clarity about the timing for an event. You can use these prepositions to explain more precisely time elements for sports events and activities, such as when a game starts or how long it lasts.

We saw some prepositions (*pendant, depuis, pour*) for expressing duration in Unit 2. Below are additional common French prepositions of time and examples of how to use them.

À – at

*Le match commence **à** 19h.* (The match starts at 7 p.m.)

En – in (used with identifiable periods, such as months or seasons)

*Ils jouent au rugby **en** automne.* (They play rugby in the fall.)

Dans – in (used for the future)

*Le tournoi commence **dans** deux semaines.* (The tournament starts in two weeks.)

Vers – around / about

*L'entraînement se terminent **vers** 18h.* (Practice ends around 6 p.m.)

De ... à – from ... to

La rencontre (d'athlétisme) est programmée __de__ 15h __à__ 17h.
(The track meet is scheduled from 3 p.m. to 5 p.m.)

Jusqu'à – until

Ils jouent au tennis __jusqu'à__ la tombée de la nuit.
(They play tennis until nightfall.)

Superlatives

When talking about sports teams and athletes, it's very common to rank them or their performances. You will find it extremely useful to know how to form the superlative form. The superlative allows you to express the extremes of any quality in French – best, worst, fastest, slowest, etc. Superlatives can indicate either superiority (the most of a quality) or inferiority (the least of a quality).

Superiority

To form the superior superlative for adjectives, the grammatical structure is *le / la / les + plus + adjective*. To choose the appropriate article among *le / la / les*, you'll want to match the number and gender of the noun. The word *plus* does not change. As with the article, the adjective varies to match the number and gender of the noun. Here are some examples to clarify the agreement rules:

*Usain Bolt est **le plus rapide** sur 100 mètres.*
(Usain Bolt is the fastest in the 100 meters.)

*Simone Biles est **la plus talentueuse** en gymnastique.*
(Simone Biles is the most talented in gymnastics.)

*Rafael Nadal et Roger Federer sont **les plus agiles** sur un terrain de tennis.*
(Rafael Nadal and Roger Federer are the most agile (players) on tennis court.)

You can also form superior superlatives with adverbs. The structure is simpler: *le + plus + adverb*. There is no need to adjust the article or adverb to agree with the noun.

*Il nage **le plus rapidement** parmi les co-équipiers.*
(He swims the fastest among the teammates.)

*Elle gagne **le plus souvent**.*
(She wins most often.)

*Les footballeurs voyagent **le plus loin** pour leurs matchs.*
(The soccer players travel farthest for their matches.)

Inferiority

To form the inferior superlative for adjectives, the grammatical structure is *le / la / les + moins + adjective*. The agreement rules are the same as for the superior superlative. The article and the adjective must match the number and gender of the noun. The word *moins* does not change. These examples show the agreement rules:

*Paul est le coureur **le moins endurant** de l'équipe d'athlétisme.*
(Paul has the least endurance of any runner on the track team.)

*Jessica est **la moins expérimentée** en escrime.*
(Jessica is the least experienced in fencing.)

*Les nouvelles entraineuses sont **les moins exigeantes**.*
(The new coaches are the least demanding.)

The structure for inferior superlative adverbs is: *le + moins + adverb*. As with the superior form, there is no need to adjust the article or adverb.

*C'est lui qui parle **le moins clairement** dans l'équipe.*
(He is the one who speaks the least clearly on the team.)

*Elle court **le moins rapidement** de toutes les participantes.*
(She runs the least quickly of all the participants.)

*Ce projet a été réalisé **le moins efficacement** de toute l'année.*
(This project was carried out the least efficiently of the entire year.)

Sports Vocabulary

French term	English meaning
l'athlétisme	athletics / track & field
la natation	swimming
le tennis	tennis
la boxe	boxing
le ski	skiing
l'escrime	fencing
le cyclisme	cycling
le match	match/game
le stade	stadium
le but	goal
l'équipe	team
l'entraîneur / l'entraîneuse	coach
jouer	to play
le joueur / la joueuse	player
le ballon	ball
le maillot	jersey
l'arbitre	referee
le terrain	field/court
la tribune	the stands
le spectateur / la spectatrice	spectator
la diffusion	broadcast
le commentateur / la commentatrice	commentator

EXERCISES II

1. **Complétez chaque phrase avec la structure qui manque.**
   Complete each sentence with the missing grammatical phrase.

   a. _____ le match de rugby, il grignote.
   (While watching the rugby match, he eats snacks.)

   b. _____ l'entraînement, ils font des étirements.
   (After they finish practice, they do stretches.)

   c. _____ à la salle de sport, n'oublie pas de vérifier ton équipement.
   (Before going to the gym, don't forget to check your equipment.)

   d. _____ un lancer-franc, les fans retiennent leur souffle.
   (While he shoots a free throw, the fans hold their breath.)

   e. _____ , il se sèche avec une serviette.
   (After swimming, he dried off with a towel.)

   f. _____ au tennis, la pluie nous perturbe.
   (While we play tennis, the rain bothers us.)

   g. _____ leur match, les handballeuses ont regardé l'enregistrement.
   (After they lost their match, the (female) handball players watched the recording.)

   h. _____ au judo, nous nous saluons avec une révérence.
   (Before fighting in judo, we greet each other with a bow.)

   i. _____ de longues distances, elle écoute de la musique.
   (While running long distances, she listens to music.)

   j. _____ le tournoi, elles ont célébré avec leurs fans.
   (After winning the tournament, they celebrated with their fans.)

2. **Complétez chaque phrase avec la préposition de temps qui convient.**
   Complete each sentence with the appropriate time preposition.

   a. *Pendant la Coupe du monde, ils regardent les matchs* _____.
   (During the World Cup, they watch the games from noon to midnight.)

   b. *Le match de basket dure* _____.
   (The basketball game lasts until 11 p.m.)

   c. *Ils vont arriver au stade* _____.
   (They will arrive at the stadium in five minutes.)

   d. *Le match de handball commence* _____.
   (The handball match starts at 8 p.m.)

   e. *L'équipe commence son échauffement* _____.
   (The team begins its warm-up around 6 p.m.)

   f. _____, *nous faisons souvent du ski alpin.*
   (In winter, we often do downhill skiing.)

3. **Traduisez chaque phrase de l'anglais vers le français.**
   Translate each sentence from English to French. (If you do not know a word, look it up.)

   a. The player with number 12 on her jersey is the fastest.
   _____

   b. The French fencers strike the most accurately.
   _____

   c. This tennis player is the least well-liked in the tournament.
   _____

   d. He plays the least often of any player in the league.
   _____

   e. The Chinese divers are the most graceful in the competition.
   _____

   f. The heavyweight is the least agile boxer.
   _____

CHAPTER 3
Crafting Hobbies

In France, people love activities like sewing, knitting, crochet, watercolor painting, scrapbooking, and even making their own jewelry. Many people spend weekend afternoons browsing in craft stores in search of inspiration for their next project. These hobbies offer an artistic outlet or sometimes a small income for serious crafters and an enjoyable distraction for many more who craft for fun. In this Chapter, you'll learn some useful terms for discussing crafting hobbies. We'll also look at quantities and prepositions of place.

Approximate Quantities

When talking about quantities, we often do not have exact measurements. Knowing expressions for approximate amounts is especially important where precision is not possible or not really desired. In crafting, for example, you might want to add "a touch" of color or you might have "a pile" of buttons. This section provides you some French terms to discuss approximate quantities so that you can give more nuance than *un peu* (a little) and *beaucoup* (a lot) allow.

Un tas de : **a lot of, a ton of** (literally "a pile of")

Elle a un tas de rubans colorés. (She has a lot of colorful ribbons.)

Quelques : **a few**

J'ai quelques boutons à coudre sur ma jupe. (I have a few buttons to sew onto my skirt.)

Un bout de : **a bit of, a piece of**

Il me faut un bout de tissu pour terminer cette poupée. (I need a piece of fabric to finish this doll.)

Une poignée de : **a handful of**

J'ai une poignée de perles pour faire un collier. (I have a handful of beads to make a necklace.)

Un morceau de : **a piece of, a scrap of**

Nous avons utilisé un morceau de papier bleu pour chaque faire-part. (We used a scrap of blue paper for each invitation.)

Un brin de : **a bit of, a strand / sprig**

Ajoutez un brin de lavande pour de la fraîcheur. (Add a sprig of lavender for a fresh sensation.)

Une pincée de : **a pinch of, a touch of**

Mettez une pincée de paillettes sur la carte pour de l'éclat.
(Put a pinch of glitter on the card for some sparkle.)

For terms that have similar meanings, such as *un bout de* and *un morceau de*, there are no firm rules for which to choose. Often, the choice is based on how formal the language is: *bout* is much less formal than *morceau*. In other instances, the speaker may prefer the option that sounds best. Finally, some phrases reflect the most common usage. A few of these common usage phrases are below:

French term	English meaning
un tas de choses à faire	a lot of things to do
quelques minutes	a few minutes
un bout de papier	a scrap of paper
un morceau de gâteau	a piece of cake (literal meaning)
une pincée de sel	a pinch of salt
un brin de vérité	a hint / grain of truth
un brin de magie	a touch of magic

Prepositions of Place

Prepositions of place are words that indicate the position of a person or thing in relation to something else. These prepositions are helpful for describing where something is located. For these prepositions, whether one word or a prepositional phrase, you use them after the conjugated verb (often *être* or *se trouver*) and before the noun that relates to the location.

Let's explore a few of the more common French prepositions of place with examples that demonstrate how to use them.

Sur : on

La boîte est sur la table. (The box is on the table.)

Les ciseaux se trouvent sur l'étagère. (The scissors are on the shelf.)

Sous : under

L'aiguille est tombée sous la chaise. (The needle fell under the chair.)

Les pinceaux sont sous le chevalet. (The brushes are under the easel.)

Dans : in

Le tissu est dans le tiroir. (The fabric is in the drawer.)

Les perles sont dans le coffre. (The beads are in the box.)

Devant : in front of

La machine à coudre est devant la chaise. (The sewing machine is in front of the chair.)

Le chevalet est devant la fenêtre. (The easel is in front of the window.)

Derrière : behind

Le coffre-fort se trouve derrière le tableau. (The safe is behind the painting.)

Les fournitures de peinture sont derrière l'armoire. (The painting supplies are behind the cabinet.)

Entre : between

La règle est entre les ciseaux et la colle. (The ruler is between the scissors and the glue.)

Le croquis est entre les pinceaux et les crayons. (The sketch is between the brushes and the pencils.)

À côté de : next to

Les boutons sont à côté de la boîte à couture. (The buttons are next to the sewing box.)

La palette est à côté des pinceaux. (The palette is next to the brushes.)

Près de : near

Les bobines se trouvent près de la machine à coudre. (The thread spools are near the sewing machine.)

Les crochets sont près des pelotes de laine. (The crochet hooks are near the balls of yarn.)

Crafting Vocabulary

French term	English meaning
la couture	sewing
coudre	to sew
le crochet	crochet
le tricot	knitting
la broderie	embroidery
la tapisserie (à l'aguille)	needlepoint
la peinture	painting (as an activity)
le tableau	painting (as an object)
le dessin	drawing
le croquis	sketch
le scrapbooking	scrapbooking
les fournitures	supplies
un atelier	workshop, studio

EXERCISES III

1. **Complétez chaque phrase avec la quantité approximative qui convient le mieux.**
   Complete each sentence with the approximate quantity that fits best.

   a. *Il a trouvé _____ points de crochet intéressants à essayer.*
   (He found a few interesting crochet stitches to try.)

   b. *Elle a utilisé _____ boutons pour décorer son châle.*
   (She used a handful of buttons to decorate her shawl.)

   c. *Avec _____ couleur, le tableau va paraître moins sombre.*
   (With a touch of color, the painting will look less dark.)

   d. *Il y a _____ laines différentes dans cette boutique.*
   (There are a ton of different yarns in this shop.)

   e. *On peut utiliser _____ tissu pour réparer ce trou.*
   (We can use a piece of cloth to mend this hole.)

   f. *Il nous faut _____ fermoirs pour les bracelets.*
   (We need a few clasps for the bracelets.)

   g. *_____ fil doré peut embellir votre création.*
   (A strand of golden thread could embellish your creation.)

   h. *Le couturier a mis _____ ruban pour une touche élégante.*
   (The tailor added a piece of ribbon for an elegant touch.)

   i. *Elle a besoin d'_____ éponge pour estomper les contours de l'aquarelle.*
   (She needs a piece of sponge to soften the contours of the watercolor painting.)

   j. *_____ sable va ajouter du relief à votre tableau.*
   (A pinch of sand will add texture to your painting.)

2. **Complétez chaque phrase avec la préposition de place qui convient.**
   Complete each sentence with the appropriate preposition of place.

   a. *Les aiguilles à tricoter sont _____ l'étagère.*
      (The knitting needles are <u>on</u> the shelf.)

   b. *Le carton est _____ la table de bricolage.*
      (The cardboard is <u>under</u> the craft table.)

   c. *Les tissus sont _____ l'armoire.*
      (The fabrics are <u>in</u> the cabinet.)

   d. *Le tableau est _____ la fenêtre.*
      (The painting is <u>in front of</u> the window.)

   e. *Les fournitures de bijouterie sont _____ la porte.*
      (The jewelry-making supplies are <u>near</u> the door.)

   f. *Les pinceaux sont _____ les craies de couleurs.*
      (The brushes are <u>behind</u> the colored chalk.)

   g. *La colle est _____ les ciseaux et les boutons.*
      (The glue is <u>between</u> the scissors and the buttons.)

   h. *Le livre des patrons est _____ la machine à coudre.*
      (The pattern book is <u>next to</u> the sewing machine.)

3. Écoutez la narration suivante au sujet de la mosaïque. Remplissez les blancs avec les mots manquants.
Listen to the following narration about mosaics. Fill in the blanks with the missing words.

[English translation is below]

Mon hobby préféré est la création de cadres en mosaïque. J'adore travailler avec des différentes couleurs et textures des tesselles. J'ai toujours _____ vieilles assiettes _____ ma table de travail.

Pour commencer, je choisis un cadre en bois et je casse _____ assiettes pour créer des tesselles uniques. Ensuite, je colle _____ chaque couleur en utilisant une pince. Souvent, je dois chercher _____ morceaux cassés _____ ma boîte à fournitures qui se trouve _____ la table.

Les colles et mes outils sont toujours _____ cadre, prêts à être utilisés. Parfois, j'ajoute _____ paillettes pour donner un coup d'éclat. À la fin, je mets le cadre _____ la fenêtre pour le faire sécher.

Créer des cadres en mosaïque est une activité relaxante et gratifiante pour moi.

My favorite hobby is making mosaic picture frames. I love working with different colors and textures of tiles. I always have a pile of old plates on my worktable.

To start, I select a wooden frame and then break a few plates to create unique tiles. Then, I glue a piece of each color (to the frame) using pliers. I often have to look for a handful of broken pieces in my supply box under the table.

I always keep the glue and my tools next to the frame, ready for use. Sometimes, I add a touch of glitter for some sparkle. As a final step, I put the frame near the window to dry.

Making mosaic frames is a relaxing and rewarding activity for me.

CHAPTER 4
Volunteering

Civic engagement is an important aspect of French life. Individual volunteering and *la vie associative* are deeply rooted in French culture as they promote the value of solidarity (*la solidarité*). Volunteer and charitable organizations (*les associations*) address various social, cultural, and environmental issues, sometimes providing essential social services and support. Other *associations* focus more on shared interests, such as school alumni organizations or common geographic backgrounds, fostering camaraderie, and belonging. Many French people belong to one or more *associations*. So, understanding *la vie associative* can be helpful in everyday conversations.

This chapter focuses on the present subjunctive and how to speak about certainty and doubt in French.

Present Subjunctive

In French, the present subjunctive (*le subjonctif présent*) is a verb mood for expressing doubt / possibility, necessity / obligation, impressions, and wants. The subjunctive mood contrasts with the indicative mood, which, as we saw earlier in this Unit, is used to provide factual information.

Conjugation

For the present subjunctive for **regular verbs**, the third person plural (*ils / elles*) present tense conjugation serves as a reference point. To form the present subjunctive, you need to know two key things: (1) the third person plural conjugation of the verb, and (2) the respective "new" endings for the subjunctive.

For all regular verb groups, the subjunctive endings are: *-e*, *-es*, *-e*, *-ions*, *-iez*, and *-ent*.

Starting from the third person plural form of the present tense, you drop the *-ent* at the end to obtain your stem. You then add the appropriate subjunctive ending to this stem. Below are examples for the regular verb categories.

-er verbs

parler	Present third person plural: *ils / elles* par<u>lent</u>				
je par<u>le</u>	tu par<u>les</u>	il / elle par<u>le</u>	nous par<u>lions</u>	vous par<u>liez</u>	ils / elles par<u>lent</u>

-ir verbs

finir	Present third person plural: *ils / elles* fini<u>ss</u>ent					
je finiss<u>e</u>	tu finiss<u>es</u>	il / elle finiss<u>e</u>	nous finiss<u>ions</u>	vous finiss<u>iez</u>	ils / elles finiss<u>ent</u>

-re verbs

attendre	Present third person plural: *ils / elles* attend<u>ent</u>					
j'attend<u>e</u>	tu attend<u>es</u>	il / elle attend<u>e</u>	nous attend<u>ions</u>	vous attend<u>iez</u>	ils / elles attend<u>ent</u>

You may notice that for *-er* verbs, the singular forms and the third person plural form of the present subjunctive look identical to the regular present tense. The same is true for the third personal plural subjunctive for *-re* verbs. When reading or listening, the context will indicate that the verb form is the subjunctive. This similarity makes learning the subjunctive for those forms a little easier.

For **irregular verbs**, forming the subjunctive is more difficult. While some irregular verbs use the third person present plural form as the subjunctive stem, others have a different (and not always obvious) stem. You'll need to look up a specific irregular verb. Below are the present subjunctive forms for verbs you're likely to need.

être (to be)	*avoir* (to have)	*aller* (to go)	*faire* (to do / make)	*savoir* (to know)
je sois	j'aie	j'aille	je fasse	je sache
tu sois	tu aies	tu ailles	tu fasses	tu saches
il / elle soit	il / elle ait	il / elle aille	il / elle fasse	il / elle sache
nous soyons	nous ayons	nous allions	nous fassions	nous sachions
vous soyez	vous ayez	vous alliez	vous fassiez	vous sachiez
ils / elles soient	ils / elles aient	ils / elles aillent	ils / elles fassent	ils / elles sachent

When to Use

Let's look more closely at the contexts that call for you to use the subjunctive. As mentioned above, we divide these into four main categories: (1) doubt / possibility, (2) necessity / obligation, (3) impressions, and (4) wants. You will need the subjunctive in relative clauses that follow verbs that express these moods.

Expressing doubt, possibility, or uncertainty:

Je doute que l'association <u>réalise</u> ses objectifs sans plus de volontaires.
(I doubt that the association will reach its goals without more volunteers.)

Penses-tu que les bénévoles <u>aillent</u> faire une réelle différence en si peu de temps ?
(Do you think that the volunteers are going to make a real difference in such a short time?)

Indicating necessity or obligation:

Il est essentiel que nous <u>trouvions</u> plus de fonds pour soutenir ce projet.
(It's essential that we find more funds to support this project.)

Il faut que vous <u>travailliez</u> ensemble pour le succès de l'association.
(You must work together for the success of the association.)

Conveying personal impressions (such as emotions or feelings):

Je suis ravie que tu <u>viennes</u> à notre événement caritatif.
(I am thrilled that you are coming to our charity event.)

Nous sommes surpris que tant de gens <u>souhaitent</u> aider l'association cette année.
(We are surprised that so many people want to help the association this year.)

Expressing wants (wishes or commands):

Elle souhaite que vous <u>apportiez</u> votre soutien à cette cause.
(She wants you to / She wishes that you would lend your support to this cause.)

Le président exige que nous <u>réunissions</u> tous les membres pour une réunion.
(The president requires us to gather all the members for a meeting.)

Discussing Certainty & Doubt

Now that we understand the subjunctive, we can begin to introduce more nuanced discussions of certainty and doubt into conversation. These two mindsets correspond to the indicative and subjunctive verb moods.

Certainty

French typically uses the indicative mood for expressing certainty because the indicative conveys statements of fact or beliefs the speaker perceives to be true. Here are some common expressions of certainty with examples of how you might use them.

Il est certain que (It is certain that...)

Il est certain que l'association aide beaucoup de gens.
(It is certain that the association helps a lot of people.)

Je suis sûr(e) que (I am sure that...)

Je suis sûr(e) que nous allons réussir notre collecte de fonds.
(I am sure that we will succeed in our fundraising.)

Il est évident que (It is obvious that...)

Il est évident que les bénévoles sont essentiels.
(It is obvious that volunteers are essential.)

Il est clair que (It is clear that...)

Il est clair que vous devez rallier notre cause.
(It is clear that you must join our cause.)

Doubt

In contrast, expressing doubt or uncertainty typically uses the subjunctive mood, which emphasizes the subjective impressions or emotions that underlie the statement. Let's explore some common French phrases for expressing uncertainty along with examples.

Je doute que **(I doubt that...)**

Je doute que nous ayons assez de fonds pour ce projet.
(I doubt that we have enough funds for this project.)

Il est possible que / c'est possible que **(It is possible that...)**

Il est possible que vous ne trouviez pas de bénévoles pour demain.
(It is possible that you won't find volunteers for tomorrow.)

Je ne pense / crois pas **(I do not think / believe that...)** *

Je ne pense pas que nous distribuions assez de nourriture.
(I don't think we distribute enough food.)

Penses-tu / Pensez-vous que **(Do you think that...)** *

Penses-tu que l'association réussisse sans plus de soutien ?
(Do you think that the association will succeed without more support?)

* Note that when you use *penser* or *croire* in the affirmative, the French consider that it expresses certainty. So, you use the indicative rather than the subjunctive mood.

Volunteer and Charity Vocabulary

French term	English meaning
association	club or volunteer organization
caritatif	charitable
bénévole / volontaire	volunteer
bénévolat	volunteering
campagne	campaign
collecte de fonds	fundraising
dons	donations
cause	cause
soutien	support
solidarité	solidarity
projet	project
distribution	distribution
secours	assistance
aide alimentaire	food aid
aide humanitaire	humanitarian aid
sensibilisation	awareness

✏️ EXERCISES IV

1. **Pour chaque verbe, donnez la conjugaison du subjonctif demandée.**
   For each verb, fill in the correct conjugation of the subjunctive.

   a. *aider* (to help): *vous* _____

   b. *participer* (to participate): *ils* _____

   c. *soutenir* (to support): *je* _____

   d. *contribuer* (to contribute): *nous* _____

   e. *organiser* (to organize): *on* _____

   f. *encourager* (to encourage): *tu* _____

   g. *collecter* (to collect (funds, donations)): *elles* _____

   h. *distribuer* (to distribute): *il* _____

   i. *sensibiliser* (to raise awareness): *nous* _____

   j. *se réunir* (to meet): *vous* _____

2. **Pour chaque phrase, complétez avec le présent de l'indicatif ou le subjonctif selon le contexte.**
   Complete each sentence with either the present indicative or subjunctive based on the context.
   (If you don't know the word or the subjunctive stem, look it up.)

   a. *Il est évident que l'engagement des volontaires _____ la communauté.*
      (It is obvious that the volunteers' commitment helps the community.)

   b. *Est-il possible que nous _____ l'événement ?*
      (Is it possible that we postpone the event?)

   c. *Il est certain que la collecte de fonds _____ réussir cette année.*
      (It is certain that the fundraising drive is going to succeed this year.)

   d. *Elle n'est pas sûre que ce projet _____ réalisable sans aide extérieure.*
      (She is not sure that this project is feasible without external help.)

   e. *Je suis convaincue que tous les bénévoles _____ beaucoup de satisfaction personnelle.*
      (I am convinced that all the volunteers experience a lot of personal satisfaction.)

   f. *Pensez-vous que nous _____ assez de ressources pour lancer ce projet ?*
      (Do you think that we have enough resources to launch this project?)

   g. *Il est clair que l'association _____ grâce au soutien des membres.*
      (It is clear that the association operates thanks to the support of its members.)

   h. *Je doute que nous _____ organiser l'événement à temps.*
      (I doubt that we can organize the event on time.)

   i. *Ils croient que leur association _____ un travail remarquable.*
      (They believe their association does remarkable work.)

   j. *Il est peu probable que chaque membre _____ les statuts.*
      (It is unlikely that every member understands the bylaws.)

UNIT 5
MEMORIES, WISHES, AND PLANS

In Unit 5, you will learn to look backward and to look forward as we learn how to discuss memories, wishes, and plans. We introduce two new verb tenses for describing the past and grammatical structures for envisioning an ideal present or planning the near future.

CHAPTER 1
Memories

Being able to discuss childhood memories adds richness to conversations and relationships. While the perfect tense works for certain memories, the imperfect tense works better for many other past situations. Also, unless you're like the famous singer who had too few regrets to mention, you may find it helpful to be able to discuss things you might have done differently.

Imperfect Tense

In French, the imperfect tense is used to describe (1) actions that used to happen regularly in the past (known as "habitual actions"), (2) actions that happened during a continuous period in the past (known as "ongoing actions"), (3) descriptions of past states or conditions, and (4) setting the scene in storytelling.

Conjugation

For **regular verbs** in the imperfect tense, the first-person plural (*nous*) present tense conjugation serves as a reference point. To form the imperfect, you need to know two things: (1) the first-person plural conjugation of the verb and (2) the respective "new" endings for the imperfect tense.

 The imperfect endings are: *-ais, -ais, -ait, -ions, -iez, -aient*.

Starting from the first-person plural form of the present tense, you drop the *-ons* at the end to obtain your stem. You then add the appropriate imperfect ending to this stem. Below are examples for the regular verb categories.

-er verbs

parler	Present first-person plural: *nous parlons*				
je parl<u>ais</u>	tu parl<u>ais</u>	il / elle parl<u>ait</u>	nous parl<u>ions</u>	vous parl<u>iez</u>	ils / elles parl<u>aient</u>

-ir verbs

finir	Present first-person plural: *nous finissons*				
je finiss<u>ais</u>	tu finiss<u>ais</u>	il / elle finiss<u>ait</u>	nous finiss<u>ions</u>	vous finiss<u>iez</u>	ils / elles finiss<u>aient</u>

-re verbs

attendre	Present first-person plural: *nous attend<u>ons</u>*				
j'attend<u>ais</u>	tu attend<u>ais</u>	il / elle attend<u>ait</u>	nous attend<u>ions</u>	vous attend<u>iez</u>	ils / elles attend<u>aient</u>

You may notice that the first and second-person plural forms of the imperfect look identical to the subjunctive present tense. When reading or listening, the context will indicate whether the verb form is the imperfect or the subjunctive. If it discusses a subjective impression or an uncertainty in the present, it is most likely the subjunctive mood. If it describes the past, it is mostly likely the imperfect tense.

For **irregular verbs**, for all except one verb, to form the imperfect, you use the same process of (1) looking to the *nous* form for the stem, (2) dropping the *-ons*, and (3) adding the same set of endings.

The only verb that does not follow the "*nous* rule" is **être**. Rather than beginning with *nous sommes*, the stem for **être** in the imperfect is *ét-*. The full conjugation is below:

être (to be)	
j'**étais**	nous **étions**
tu **étais**	vous **étiez**
il / elle **était**	ils / elles **étaient**

When to Use

As mentioned above, four contexts demand the imperfect: (1) past habitual actions, (2) ongoing past actions, (3) descriptions of past states, and (4) background for stories.

Habitual actions:

Pendant mon enfance, <u>je jouais</u> dans le parc tous les jours.
(During my childhood, I played in the park every day.)

Note: You could also say "I used to play in the park every day." When "used to" can be implied, the imperfect tense is the correct tense.

Nous allions chez nos grands-parents chaque été.
(We went to our grandparents' house every summer.)

Ongoing past actions:

Il lisait un livre quand tu as appelé.
(He was reading a book when you called.)

Note: When one action is interrupted by another, the imperfect is typically the correct tense for the interrupted action.

Nous faisions un château de sable quand la vague s'est déferlée sur nous.
(We were making a sandcastle when the wave crashed down on us.)

Descriptions of past states (conditions, emotions):

Le terrain de jeu était toujours animé et bondé.
(The playground was always lively and crowded.)

La maison se trouvait au bord d'un lac.
(The house was on a lakefront.)

Elles étaient très heureuses.
(They were very happy.)

Note: For discussing past emotions, the imperfect is typically the correct tense.

Background information:

Il faisait beau, et les oiseaux chantaient.
(It was a sunny day, and the birds were singing.)

On venait de découvrir un trésor caché.
(They had just discovered a hidden treasure.)

Discussing Regrets

Reminiscing about childhood can bring up memories of things we might have done or done differently "if only...". To express regrets in French, the verb phrase is **regretter de** + **infinitive**. This structure is straightforward in the present, but let's confirm our understanding with a couple of examples:

Nous regrettons de vous informer de notre départ.
(We regret to inform you of our departure.)

Il regrette de ne pas passer plus de temps avec ses enfants.
(He regrets not spending more time with his children.)

When talking about past regrets two potential complications come up. First, you need to use the infinitive of *être* or *avoir* as an auxiliary verb and the past participle of the main verb. The structure is **regretter d'** + être / **avoir** + **past participle of main verb**. Second, this structure is often followed by a relative clause beginning with *quand* that requires the imperfect. Here are a few examples:

*Elle regrette d'avoir mangé autant de sucreries quand elle **était** enfant.*
(She regrets eating so many sweets when she was a child.)

Je regrette d'avoir passé tant de temps à l'intérieur quand il faisait beau.
(I regret spending so much time indoors when the weather was nice.)

You can often avoid *quand* relative clauses by using a preposition of time and a noun. The two examples above could instead become:

Elle regrette d'avoir mangé autant de sucreries pendant son enfance.
(She regrets eating so many sweets during her childhood.)

Je regrette d'avoir passé tant de temps à l'intérieur durant les beaux jours.
(I regret spending so much time indoors when the weather was nice.)

Note: We'll explore how to express past regrets using the conditional tense in the next chapter.

Childhood and Vacation Vocabulary

French term	English meaning
le jouet	toy
le jeu	game
terrain de jeu	playground
cache-cache	hide-and-seek
toboggan	slide
balançoire	swing
bac à sable	sand box
le manège	merry-go-round
colonie de vacances	summer camp
carte postale	postcard
se souvenir de	to remember
souvenir	memory
la nostalgie	nostalgia

EXERCISES I

1. **Pour chaque verbe, donnez la conjugaison de l'imparfait demandée.**
   For each verb, fill in the correct conjugation of the imperfect tense.

   a. *jouer* (to play): *elles* _____

   b. *courir* (to run): *tu* _____

   c. *sauter* (to jump): *je* _____

   d. *nager* (to swim): *nous* _____

   e. *rire* (to laugh): *il* _____

   f. *dessiner* (to draw): *vous* _____

   g. *rêver* (to dream): *on* _____

   h. *explorer* (to explore): *elle* _____

   i. *se déguiser* (to dress up): *ils* _____

   j. *construire* (to build): *tu* _____

2. **Pour chaque phrase, complétez avec le passé composé ou l'imparfait selon le contexte.**
   Complete each sentence with either the present perfect or the imperfect tense, based on the context. (If you don't know the word, look it up.)

   a. *Je/J'* _____ *au football hier.*
   (I won at soccer yesterday.)

   b. *Il* _____ *des dessins animés chaque matin.*
   (He used to watch cartoons every morning.)

   c. *Tu* _____ *de ton vélo l'été dernier.*
   (You fell off your bike last summer.)

   d. *J'* _____ *à jouer à cache-cache ce matin.*
   (I learned to play hide-and-seek this morning.)

   e. *Nous* _____ *visite à nos grands-parents chaque été.*
   (We visited our grandparents every summer.)

f. Vous _____ dans le bac à sable la semaine dernière.
(You played in the sandbox last week.)

g. Elle _____ chaque après-midi.
(She painted every afternoon.)

h. Ils _____ toujours sur la cage à poule pendant la récréation.
(They always climbed on the jungle gym during recess.)

i. Nous _____ voler des cerfs-volants à la plage.
(We used to fly kites at the beach.)

j. On _____ jouer à chat perché avec mes cousins.
(My cousins and I loved playing tag.)

3. **Traduisez chaque phrase de l'anglais vers le français.**
   Translate each sentence from English to French. (If you do not know a word, look it up.)

a. He regrets saying mean things to his friends.

_____

b. I regret not studying more when I was in high school.

_____

c. Do you (*tu*) regret staying in your hometown?

_____

d. We regret moving to the suburbs.

_____

e. You are not going to regret buying this book.

_____

f. They regretted not going to bed earlier.

_____

CHAPTER 2
The Future

This chapter presents some options for talking about the future in French. We'll cover how to discuss upcoming projects and plans and present your next big idea. You'll learn to talk about what lies ahead, with confidence in your French.

Intentions and Plans

In this section, we'll explore how to express future intentions and plans in French using the phrases *envisager de* (to consider / plan to) and *avoir l'intention de* (to intend to). These expressions will help you discuss near-term projects. They allow you to add more nuance than the structure *aller* + infinitive, which we learned in Unit 2 for talking about the near future (le *futur proche*).

The good news is that these structures work in the same way as *aller* + infinitive. You conjugate the main verb – *envisager* or *avoir* – and add the infinitive form of the verb after the word *de*.

Here are some examples for both phrases.

>*J'envisage de voyager en France l'année prochaine.*
>(I'm considering traveling to France next year.)

>*Nous envisageons de lancer un nouveau produit l'année prochaine.*
>(We plan to launch a new product next year.)

>*Il a l'intention de célébrer son anniversaire à la fin du mois.*
>(He intends to celebrate his birthday at the end of the month.)

>*Elles ont l'intention de terminer tous les rapports financiers avant la réunion.*
>(They intend to finish all the financial reports before the meeting.)

The Simple Future Tense

Let's now focus on the simple future tense. In French, *le futur simple* is used to describe actions that you believe will happen later. You can use it for making plans, setting goals (slightly firmer than intentions), and forecasting future events.

How to Form

Let's explore how to form the simple future tense. You need to know two things: (1) the future stem of the verb and (2) the respective endings for each subject / pronoun.

To form the future stem, for regular verbs that end in *-er* or *-ir*, it is very simple: the future stem is just the infinitive form of the verb. For regular verbs that end in *-re*, you form the future stem by taking the infinitive and removing the "e" at the end.

The respective endings for the future tense are: *-ai, -as, -a, -ons, -ez*, and *-ont*. Some French learners find it easy to remember the simple future tense endings by seeing how they relate to the present tense of the verb *avoir* (a conjugation you can probably do in your sleep by now): *j'**ai**, tu **as**, il/elle/on **a**, nous av**ons**, vous av**ez**, ils/elles **ont**.*

Below are examples of the simple future tense for the regular verb categories.

-er verbs

parler	Future stem: *parler*				
je parler*ai*	tu parler*as*	il / elle parler*a*	nous parler*ons*	vous parler*ez*	ils / elles parler*ont*

-ir verbs

finir	Future stem: *finir*				
je finir*ai*	tu finir*as*	il / elle finir*a*	nous finir*ons*	vous finir*ez*	ils / elles finir*ont*

-re verbs

attendre	Future stem: *attendr(e)*				
j'attendr*ai*	tu attendr*as*	il / elle attendr*a*	nous attendr*ons*	vous attendr*ez*	ils / elles attendr*ont*

For **irregular verbs**, forming the simple future tense is slightly more difficult because the future stems do not always obey the above rules. As there are no uniform rules for irregular verbs, you'll need to look up the specific irregular verb you want to use. Below are the simple forms for common irregular verbs.

être (to be) Future stem: *ser-*	*avoir* (to have) Future stem: *aur-*	*aller* (to go) Future stem: *ir-*	*faire* (to do / make) Future stem: *fer-*	*savoir* (to know) Future stem: *saur-*
je serai	j'aurai	j'irai	je ferai	je saurai
tu seras	tu auras	tu iras	tu feras	tu sauras
il / elle sera	il / elle aura	il / elle ira	il / elle fera	il / elle saura
nous serons	nous aurons	nous irons	nous ferons	nous saurons
vous serez	vous aurez	vous irez	vous ferez	vous saurez
ils / elles seront	ils / elles auront	ils / elles iront	ils / elles feront	ils / elles sauront

When to Use

As mentioned above, you can use the simple future tense to discuss plans, set objectives, or make promises or predictions about what will happen. Here are some examples:

Elles participeront à la conférence l'année prochaine.
(They will attend the conference next year.)

Nous terminerons la recherche ce trimestre.
(We will complete the research this quarter.)

Je présenterai notre nouvelle application lors de la réunion.
(I will present our new app at the meeting.)

Le marché évoluera vers des solutions durables.
(The market will shift toward sustainable solutions.)

Notre nouvelle voiture réduira vos dépenses en carburant de moitié.
(Our new car will cut your gas spending in half.)

EXERCISES II

1. **Écoutez la conversation suivante entre Marie et Paul. Lisez d'abord le texte pendant que vous l'écoutez. Ensuite, lisez à voix haute durant votre deuxième écoute.**
   Listen to the following conversation between Marie and Paul. First, read the script as you listen to it, and then try to read it aloud as you listen a second time.

[English translation below]

Marie: *Bonjour Paul, tu as des projets pour l'année prochaine ?*

Paul: *Oui, j'ai l'intention de changer de travail. J'envisage de postuler pour un poste à l'étranger.*

Marie: *C'est génial ! Et tu as d'autres plans ?*

Paul: *Oui, avec ma famille, nous envisageons de déménager en Espagne. Et toi, quels sont tes projets ?*

Marie: *J'ai l'intention de finir mon master en marketing. Ensuite, j'envisage de lancer ma propre entreprise.*

Paul: *Super ! Je suis sûr que tu réussiras.*

Marie: Hi Paul, do you have any plans for next year?

Paul: Yes, I intend to change jobs. I'm considering applying for a position abroad.

Marie: That's great! And do you have any other plans?

Paul: Yes, with my family, we are planning to move to Spain. And you, what are your plans?

Marie: I intend to finish my master's in marketing. Then, I'm considering starting my own business.

Paul: Awesome! I'm sure you will succeed.

French Made Easy Level 2 | Unit 5

2. Pour chaque verbe, donnez la conjugaison du futur simple.
For each verb, fill in the correct conjugation of the simple future tense.

a. *décider* (to decide): *ils* _____

b. *investir* (to invest): *j'* _____

c. *augmenter* (to increase): *le marché* _____

d. *lancer* (to launch): *nous* _____

e. *préparer* (to prepare): *vous* _____

f. *organiser* (to organize): *tu* _____

g. *développer* (to develop): *elle* _____

h. *atteindre* (to reach): *les ventes* _____

i. *voir* (to see): *on* _____

j. *faire* (to do): *vous* _____

CHAPTER 3
Hopes and Dreams

Connecting with others by discussing hopes and dreams can help build deeper relationships. When you can exchange about your aspirations – whether career goals, travel plans, or personal achievements (like becoming fluent in French) – you may find support, encouragement, and inspiration. This chapter focuses on grammar and vocabulary to help you share your present and past ambitions.

Conditional Tense: Overview

We use the conditional tense to express dreams, wishes, and possibilities. When we talk about what might have happened (in the past), what could happen, or what we wish would happen, we are using the conditional tense.

In English, the word "if" in a sentence usually signals that we'll find the conditional tense either in the dependent "if" (condition) clause or in the independent (results) clause. The explicit "if" clause is not a requirement, but English does require using "would," "could," or "might" to express conditionality. For example, "I would if I could" or "If I had known, I might have come" or "I could have been a contender."

In French, the conditional tense applies in the same contexts, but instead of having designated verbs it has a special conjugation. We'll learn the present conditional and the past conditional in this section.

Present Conditional

To express a possibility or discuss a dream or wish, you use the present conditional.

How to Form

For the present conditional tense for **regular verbs**, you need to know two things: (1) the future stem of the verb (refer to Chapter 2 of this unit) and (2) the respective "new" endings for the conditional tense. The conditional endings are not actually "new" as they are identical to the imperfect endings: *-ais, -ais, -ait, -ions, -iez, -aient*.

Below are examples of the present conditional tense for the regular verb categories. Again, it is formed by taking the stem for the future tense and adding the endings for the imperfect tense (-*ais*, -*ais*, -*ait*, -*ions*, -*iez*, -*aient*).

-er verbs

parler	Future stem: *parler*				
je parler<u>ais</u>	tu parler<u>ais</u>	il / elle parler<u>ait</u>	nous parler<u>ions</u>	vous parler<u>iez</u>	ils / elles parler<u>aient</u>

-ir verbs

finir	Future stem: *finir*				
je finir<u>ais</u>	tu finir<u>ais</u>	il / elle finir<u>ait</u>	nous finir<u>ions</u>	vous finir<u>iez</u>	ils / elles finir<u>aient</u>

-re verbs

attendre	Future stem: *attendr(e)*				
j'attendr<u>ais</u>	tu attendr<u>ais</u>	il / elle attendr<u>ait</u>	nous attendr<u>ions</u>	vous attendr<u>iez</u>	ils / elles attendr<u>aient</u>

For **irregular verbs**, forming the present conditional tense is slightly more difficult because, as you may remember, the future stems do not always obey the above rules. Once you've mastered the future tense, you may have the irregular stems memorized. If not, you'll need to look up the specific irregular verb. Below are the present conditional forms for common irregular verbs. (Hint: Pay special attention to **être** and *avoir* as they will come in handy shortly.)

être (to be) Future stem: *ser-*	*avoir* (to have) Future stem: *aur-*	*aller* (to go) Future stem: *ir-*	*faire* (to do / make) Future stem: *fer-*	*savoir* (to know) Future stem: *saur-*
je serais	*j'aurais*	*j'irais*	*je ferais*	*je saurais*
tu serais	*tu aurais*	*tu irais*	*tu ferais*	*tu saurais*
il / elle serait	*il / elle aurait*	*il / elle irait*	*il / elle ferait*	*il / elle saurait*
nous serions	*nous aurions*	*nous irions*	*nous ferions*	*nous saurions*
vous seriez	*vous auriez*	*vous iriez*	*vous feriez*	*vous sauriez*
ils / elles seraient	*ils / elles auraient*	*ils / elles iraient*	*ils / elles feraient*	*ils / elles sauraient*

When to Use

As mentioned above, you use the present conditional to express possibilities or wishes. Here are some examples:

Possibilities (Might / Could Happen)

Si j'avais plus de temps, je lirais davantage.
(If I had more time, I might / could read more.)

Si jamais il faisait beau demain, nous irions à la plage.
(If the weather is nice tomorrow, we might go to the beach.)

Note: In the conditional (*si*) clause, you use the imperfect tense. You use the conditional tense in the results clause. It expresses what could happen if the condition were true.

Wishes (Would Like to Happen)

Je voudrais visiter le Japon un jour.
(I would like to visit Japan one day.)

Elle aimerait devenir une artiste célèbre.
(She would like to become a famous artist.)

Past Conditional

The past conditional is used to discuss hopes and dreams that did not quite work out. These may be hypothetical situations or regrets.

Conjugation

Forming the past conditional is straightforward. The structure is similar to the present perfect tense (*passé composé*) as it uses *avoir* or ***être*** as an auxiliary verb. The difference is that, instead of conjugating the auxiliary verb in the simple past tense, you conjugate it in the conditional tense. The full structure is:

subject/pronoun + conjugated auxiliary verb + past participle of the main verb

To form the past conditional, you need to know the conditional tense of either *avoir* or *être* and the past participle of the main verb. As with the perfect tense, for the *être* (remember our friends DR & MRS VANDERTRAMP) verbs, the past participle needs to agree with the subject.

When to Use

As mentioned above, you use the past conditional to describe hypothetical past situations (what might have been) or regrets. Here are some examples:

Hypothetical Scenarios

En travaillant dur, tu aurais eu plus de succès.
(By working hard, you would have had more success.)

Elle serait probablement devenue médecin avec plus d'encouragement.
(She would probably have become a doctor with more encouragement.)

Past Regrets

Nous aurions voulu partir en voyage en juillet.
(We would have liked to go on a trip last July.)

Il aurait aimé avoir plus de liberté à poursuivre ses rêves.
(He would have liked to have more freedom to pursue his dreams.)

To express past regrets, as an alternative to *regretter de*, you can use the structure:

subject/pronoun + conditional conjugation of *avoir* (as auxiliary verb) + *aimé* / *voulu* + infinitive

One of the most famous examples of this past regrets structure is the song *Le Blues du Businessman* (*J'aurais voulu être un artiste*) from the rock opera *Starmania*. The title translates to "The Businessman's Blues (I would have liked to be a performer)." Many artists have covered the song, including international superstar Céline Dion.

Hopes

While you can use the verbs *aimer* (to like) and *vouloir* (to want) to express past regrets, they are also useful for discussing hopes and wishes along with a third verb *espérer* (to hope). The structure is: subject/pronoun + conjugated *aimer* / *espérer* / *vouloir* + infinitive.

Let's look at present and present conditional examples for each verb.

Aimer (to like)

In the present tense, *aimer* (to like) can describe implicit wishes. In the present conditional, it describes aspirations more explicitly.

Present Tense:

J'aime apprendre de nouvelles choses.
(I like learning new things.)

Elle aime passer du temps avec ses amis.
(She likes spending time with her friends.)

Present Conditional:

J'aimerais travailler à l'étranger un jour.
(I would like to work abroad one day.)

Nous aimerions assister à plus de concerts en direct.
(We would like to attend / go to more live concerts.)

Espérer (to hope)

When expressing wishes using the verb *espérer*, the present tense expresses aspirations. The present conditional often expresses expectations or strong opinions about what should happen.

Present Tense:

Les étudiants espèrent trouver des emplois bien rémunérés.
(The students hope to find well-paying jobs.)

Nous espérons que la paix sera rétablie.
(We hope that peace will be restored.)

Present Conditional:

J'espérerais récupérer les affaires que tu m'as empruntées.
(I expect / would hope to get back the things you borrowed from me.)

Elles espéreraient être récompensées pour leurs efforts.
(They would hope to be rewarded for their efforts.)

Vouloir (to want)

The verb *vouloir* can express hopes and dreams in both the present tense and the present conditional.

Present Tense:

Je veux réussir dans ma carrière.
(I want to succeed in my career.)

Voulez-vous voyager en Asie ?
(Do you want to travel in Asia?)

Present Conditional:

Nous voudrions avoir plus de temps libre.
(We would like to have more free time.)

Ils voudraient acheter une maison à la campagne.
(They would like to buy a house in the countryside.)

📝 EXERCISES III

1. **Pour chaque verbe, donnez la conjugaison du conditionnel au présent demandée.**
   For each verb, fill in the correct conjugation of the present conditional tense.

   a. *voyager* (to travel): *vous* _____

   b. *acheter* (to buy): *elle* _____

   c. *aller* (to go): *ils* _____

   d. *créer* (to create): *nous* _____

   e. *réussir* (to succeed): *tu* _____

   f. *découvrir* (to discover): *je* _____

   g. *avoir* (to have): *on* _____

   h. *travailler* (to work): *il* _____

   i. *être* (to be): *elles* _____

   j. *étudier* (to study): *nous* _____

2. **Pour chaque phrase, complétez avec la conjugaison au présent du conditionnel du verbe « être » ou « avoir » qui convient.**
   Complete each sentence with the appropriate present conditional tense conjugation of either « être » or « avoir ».

   a. Nous _____ aimé travailler ensemble.
   (We would have loved to work together.)

   b. Ils _____ allés en France pour les vacances.
   (They would have gone to France for vacation.)

   c. Tu _____ eu une carrière impressionnante.
   (You would have had an impressive career.)

   d. Elle _____ restée plus longtemps avec plus d'argent.
   (She would have stayed longer with more money.)

   e. Avec un meilleur guide, vous _____ vu tous les monuments.
   (With a better tour guide, you would have seen all the famous monuments.)

   f. J'_____ adoré découvrir de nouveaux horizons.
   (I would have loved discovering new horizons.)

   g. Ils _____ été très fiers de leur fille.
   (They would have been very proud of their daughter.)

   h. Tu _____ devenu un grand artiste à une autre époque.
   (You would have become a great artist in another era.)

   i. Sans la capitaine, elles _____ perdu tous les matchs.
   (Without the captain, they would have lost all the matches.)

   j. Je _____ sorti plus souvent.
   (I would have gone out more often.)

3. **Écrivez quelques phrases en utilisant <u>aimer</u>, <u>espérer</u> et <u>vouloir</u> au présent ou au conditionnel présent à propos d'un ou plusieurs des sujets suivants.**

   Write a few sentences using the verbs <u>aimer</u>, <u>espérer</u>, and <u>vouloir</u> in the present or present conditional tense about one or more of the following topics.

   - **Votre emploi ou carrière idéale** *(Your ideal job or career)*
   - **Une aspiration personnelle pour cette année** *(A personal goal for this year)*
   - **Vos vacances de rêve** *(Your dream vacation)*
   - **Un souhait pour la planète ou l'humanité** *(A wish for the planet or humanity)*

CONCLUSION

Félicitations ! You've made it to the end of this workbook. Take a moment to reflect on the progress you've made.

Throughout these pages, you've learned more about French grammar, picked up new words, and read about French culture. Take your time to review the sections, practice often, and try to use French as much as you can.

Remember, learning a language is a journey. Celebrate your new learning achievements and keep reaching for new levels. Whether you're new to learning French or brushing up your language skills, you now have the tools to express more complex ideas.

You can continue your journey by immersing yourself in French whenever you can. Here are some possibilities:

- Watch French movies and TV series to hear how French is spoken naturally and to pick up new words and phrases.

- Talk with native French speakers to practice your conversation skills.

- Read French books, magazines, or comic books to expand your vocabulary and explore French in different contexts, such as formal, informal, and colloquial.

- Participate in online forums or social media in French to practice writing and reading in real-life situations.

- Listen to French language music and podcasts as a fun way to improve your listening skills and to hear different accents.

Keep exploring and enjoying the beautiful French language. Bonne continuation et bon courage dans votre apprentissage !

ANSWER KEY

UNIT 1

Exercises I

1.

a. *Je **suis** sortie avec lui. (fem. subj.)*

b. *Tu **es** devenue une bonne amie. (fem. subj.)*

c. *Il **a** appelé beaucoup.*

d. *Anne **est** revenue. (fem. subj.)*

e. *Nous **avons** regardé un film ensemble.*

f. *Vous **êtes** arrivés au bon moment. (plural subj.)*

g. *Pierre et Marie **sont** allés au restaurant hier soir. (for mixed plural subj, use masc.)*

h. *Elles **sont** tombées amoureuses de lui.*

i. *Leur fille **est** née ce matin.*

j. *Les maris **sont** restés à la maison aujourd'hui.*

2.

a. *Charlotte a monté les marches.*

b. *Christophe est retourné à Paris.*

c. *Je suis née en Angleterre.*

d. *Tu as descendu le mauvais chemin.*

e. *Son épouse est morte hier.*

f. *L'homme est tombé de sa chaise.*

g. *Leurs parents sont rentrés tôt.*

h. *Il est sorti avec sa petite amie.*

i. *Nous sommes devenus un couple heureux.*

j. *Vous êtes entrés sans billets.*

Exercises II

1.

a. *Il est fâché. / Elle est fâchée.*

b. *Il est ennuyé. / Elle est ennuyée.*

c. *Il se sent courageux. / Elle se sent courageuse.*

d. *Il est calme / Elle est calme.*

e. *Il est dégoûté. / Elle est dégoûtée.*

f. *Il a hâte. / Elle a hâte.*

g. *Il est content. / Elle est contente.*

h. *Il est jaloux. / Elle est jalouse.*

i. *Il est joyeux. / Elle est joyeuse.*

j. *Il se sent aimé. / Elle se sent aimée.*

k. *Il se sent fier. / Elle se sent fière.*

l. *Il est triste. / Elle est triste.*

m. *Il a peur. / Elle a peur.*

n. *Il se sent timide. / Elle se sent timide.*

o. *Il se sent amusé. / Elle se sent amusée.*

p. *Il est étonné. / Elle est étonnée.*

q. *Il est méfiant. / Elle est méfiante.*

r. *Il est fatigué. / Elle est fatiguée.*

s. *Il est inquiet. / Elle est inquiète.*

t. *Il se sent gourmand. / Elle se sent gourmande.*

2.

a. *Christine **se sent seule**.*

b. *Les hommes **se sentent stressés** aujourd'hui.*

c. *Tu **te sens fière** de ton petit ami.*

d. *Elle **se sent nerveuse** à l'idée de partir.*

e. *Je **me sens coupable** de ne pas aider.*

f. *Ma femme **se sent souvent épuisée** après le travail.*

g. *Nous **nous sentons contents** avec notre choix.*

h. *Les étudiants **se sentent chanceux** d'avoir des boulots.*

i. *Les femmes **se sentent inspirées** à gagner.*

j. *Vous **vous sentez nostalgiques** dans cette maison.*

k. *Ils **se sentent soulagés** de toujours s'aimer.*

l. *Nous **nous sentons honorés** de vous rencontrer.*

Exercises III

1.

a. Les invités **qui** sont venus à notre réveillon du Nouvel An étaient tous ravis.

b. La tarte **que** mon cousin prépare est traditionnelle.

c. Ma marraine n'aime pas la viande **qui** est servie à Pâques.

d. Le discours **que** ma mère a prononcé pour mon anniversaire était émouvant.

e. Les amis avec **qui** nous dînons le dimanche sont très proches de la famille.

f. Le sapin de Noël **que** ma famille décore est très grand.

g. Ma cousine porte une chemise **qui** vient du Sénégal.

h. Les bonbons **que** tu distribues chaque Halloween sont délicieux.

i. Elle a écrit un livre **qui** raconte l'histoire de sa famille.

j. Mes parents construisent une maison **qu'**ils comptent léguer à mon frère.

k. La grand-mère avec **qui** je parle habite en Chine.

l. Les enfants **qui** figurent sur la photo sont mes neveux et nièces.

m. La fête **que** vous célébrez est d'origine suédoise.

n. Les chansons d'anniversaire **que** chante ma famille sont rigolotes.

o. Les enfants pour **qui** elle fait à manger sont ses filleuls.

2.

a. Mon cousin **en** a amené.

b. Son parrain **en** organise un par an.

c. J'**en** ai reçu plusieurs hier.

d. Nous nous **en** souvenons.

e. Ma belle-mère n'**en** veut plus.

f. Ses oncles **en** parlent toujours.

g. Qu'**en** pensez-vous ?

h. Ma grand-mère **en** possède trois.

i. Mon cousin **en** rêve depuis longtemps.

j. Au réveillon de Noël, nous **en** buvons.

k. Combien **en** as-tu ?

l. Elle **en** offre à tous ses prochains.

3.

a. **_Cet_** enfant est très mignon.

b. **_Cette_** maison est ancienne.

c. **_Ces_** cousines sont gentilles.

d. **_Ces_** souvenirs sont difficiles.

e. **_Ce_** dîner est copieux.

f. **_Ces_** fleurs sont magnifiques.

4.

a. Cette fille-**_ci_** fête son anniversaire.

b. Ces années-**_là_** sont passées vites.

c. Ce père-**_là_** ramène toujours des gâteaux.

d. Ces jours-**_ci_** on aime se balader en forêt.

e. Cette carte-**_là_** vient de mon grand-père.

f. Cet hôtel-**_ci_** a une grande salle de bal.

Exercises IV

1.

a. **_Ce sont_** des clients réguliers.

b. **_C'est_** un menu végétarien.

c. **_Ce sont_** des verres à eau.

d. **_C'est_** gras, les frites.

e. **_C'est_** une table qu'il faut réserver.

f. **_C'est_** le chef du restaurant.

g. **_Ce sont_** des plats copieux.

h. **_C'est_** cher, le homard.

i. **_Ce sont_** les desserts du jour.

j. **_C'est_** un serveur qui est tombé.

2.

a. **_Ce sont_** les boissons que nous avons commandées.

b. **_C'est_** ma cuisine.

c. **_C'est_** le restaurant qui a une bonne ambiance.

d. **_Ce sont_** les plats du jour.

e. **_C'est_** le serveur qui a pris notre commande.

3.

a. *Je **le** prépare.*

b. *Nous **les** avons invités.*

c. *Justine **l'**apporte.*

d. *Vous **nous** emmenez.*

e. *Mes copines **la** décorent.*

f. *Il **vous** attend à 19 heures.*

g. *Les garçons **la** mettent.*

h. *Tu **l'**as choisie.*

i. *Le serveur **nous** remercie.*

j. *Nous **les** avons rangées.*

4.

a. *Ils **leur** expliquent les règles du jeu.*

b. *Nous **te** racontons des blagues.*

c. *Elle **lui** prodigue des conseils.*
   (remember masculine and feminine use *lui*)

d. *Claire **nous** a écrit des cartes postales.*

e. *Mon père **lui** téléphone tous les jours.*

f. *Mes potes **m'**ont apporté du vin.*

g. *Tu **leur** lis tes recettes.*

h. *Jessica **nous** parle souvent de ses rêves.*

i. *Gilles **lui** emprunte un couteau.*

j. *Philippe **vous** a raconté des histoires.*

Exercises V

1.

a. *vous* (formal office)

b. *tu* (casual office)

c. *tu* (adult to child)

d. *vous* (formal office)

e. *vous* (to older adult)

f. *vous* (ambiguous situation – *vous* to be safe)

g. *tu* (at a party with friends)

h. *vous* (to a salesclerk)

2.

a. Ils travaillent souvent pour **nous**.

b. Je veux discuter du projet avec **toi**.

c. Tu peux compter sur **elles** pour le rapport annuel.

d. Ce document vient de **lui**.

e. **Toi**, tu arrives toujours à l'heure.

f. Elles sont parties à la réunion sans **moi**.

g. Mon collègue a fait livrer une lettre à **eux** hier soir.

h. **Nous**, nous sommes retournées au bureau.

i. Le grand bureau est à **vous**.

j. Nous devons collaborer avec **elle** sur ce dossier.

3.

a. Mon patron a plus hâte que **moi**. (Remember, *excité* in French can have a double meaning.)

b. Nous voyageons moins qu'**elles**.

c. Son collègue est moins fiable que **lui**.

d. Ton assistant a travaillé plus que **toi**.

e. Marc a écrit plus de lettres que **nous**.

f. Les nouveaux clients sont plus aimables qu'**eux**.

4.

a. Les frais de livraison sont **inclus** dans le prix total.

b. Tous les bureaux sont occupés, **y compris** ceux du sous-sol.

c. Tous les membres de l'équipe, **y compris** la patronne, **étaient** présents à la réunion.

d. Le résultat de ma recherche est **inclus** dans le rapport.

e. Toutes les informations nécessaires sont **incluses** dans le document.

f. Tous les clients, **y compris** les plus difficiles, ont apprécié la présentation.

5.

a. *Les formations sont obligatoires **sauf / excepté** pour les stagiaires.*
   (Either is acceptable.)

b. ***À part** le projet en cours, nous n'avons pas d'autre travail.*

c. *Tous les employés ont reçu un bonus **sauf** ceux qui ont démissionné.*
   (*Excepté* could also be used here, but the tone is a bit less formal.)

d. *Les animaux sont formellement interdits au bureau **excepté** les chiens guides.*

e. *Ils sont tous partis en vacances **sauf** Héloïse.*

f. *Tu es disponible pour des réunions en semaine **à part** quelques mercredis.*

6.

a. *Où est allé Hugo cet été ?*
   Il est allé en Espagne.
   (He went to Spain)

b. *Qu'a fait Marie pendant l'été ?*
   Marie est restée à Paris. Elle a passé du temps avec sa famille.
   (She stayed in Paris. She spent time with her family.)

c. *Que vont faire Marie et Hugo la semaine prochaine ?*
   Marie a invité Hugo à dîner. Il a accepté.
   (Marie invited Hugo to dinner. He accepted.)

UNIT 2

Exercises I

1.

- **a.** *Il est treize heures. / Il est une heure de l'après-midi.*
- **b.** *Il est dix heures moins le quart.*
- **c.** *Il est minuit.*
- **d.** *Il est deux heures et demie.*
- **e.** *Il est cinq heures dix.*
- **f.** *Il est midi.*
- **g.** *Il est dix-huit heures quinze / Il est six heures et quart du soir.*
- **h.** *Il est vingt heures quarante-cinq / Il est neuf heures moins le quart du soir.*

2.

	lundi	mardi	mercredi	jeudi	vendredi
8:00 - 9:00	Anglais	**Étude**	Français	Politiques	Anglais
9:00 - 10:00	**Philosophie**	**Maths**	Chimie	Maths	Littérature
10:00 - 11:00	Histoire-géographie	Informatique	Économie	Art oratoire	Histoire-géographie
11:00 - 12:00	Maths	Politiques	Étude	Sports	**Économie**
12:00 - 13:00	Déjeuner	Déjeuner	Déjeuner	Déjeuner	Déjeuner
13:00 - 14:00	Français	Sports	Anglais	**Arts-plastiques**	Français
14:00 - 15:00	Arts-plastiques	Littérature	Histoire-géographie	Étude	Chimie
15:00 - 16:00	Chimie	Philosophie	**Théâtre**	Philosophie	Rattrapage

3.

a. *Il étudie le français **depuis** trois ans.*

b. *Nous avons étudié l'histoire **pendant** une heure hier.*

c. *Je vais travailler à la bibliothèque **pendant** trois heures cet après-midi.*

d. *Elles enseignent dans cette école **depuis** 2019.*

e. *Ils vont faire une pause **pendant** quinze minutes.*

f. *J'ai pris des cours de musique **pendant** l'été dernier.*

4.

a. *Je **vais** étudier l'anglais en Australie.*

b. *Les écoles **vont** fermer pour l'été.*

c. *Mon enseignant **va** écrire un livre pour enfants.*

d. *Nous **allons** déjeuner après le cours de gym.*

e. *Tu **vas** beaucoup apprendre au lycée.*

f. *Vous **allez** adorer la nouvelle bibliothèque.*

Exercises II

1.

a. *Il ne faut pas courir dans les couloirs.*

b. *Il faut lire tous les livres sur la liste.*

c. *Il ne faut pas crier après le professeur.*

d. *Il faut savoir bien écrire.*

e. *Il ne faut pas oublier les instructions.*

f. *Il faut respecter les différentes perspectives.*

2.

a. Le livre **dont** il a parlé est un classique de la littérature française. (parler de)

b. Le matin **où** nous avons étudié la Révolution française était fascinant.

c. Le collégien **dont** j'ai parlé est très bavard. (parler de)

d. Le moment **où** le professeur entre, nous nous asseyons.

e. Les salles de cours **où** on trouve des tableaux blancs interactifs sont toutes occupées.

f. Le sujet **dont** nous débattons est complexe. (débattre de)

g. Le livre **dont** elle a besoin pour ce cours est très cher. (avoir besoin de)

h. Le labo **où** vous avez fait vos expériences de chimie est bien équipé.

i. L'élève **dont** les idées sont les plus innovantes va recevoir un prix.

j. Les jours **où** les profs font la grève, les écoles sont fermées.

3.

a. Jean assiste au lycée **où** le débat va avoir lieu.

b. Les étudiants **dont** les parents sont professeurs réussissent toujours au bac.

c. Le cours de français **dont** le prof est un écrivain connu est très demandé.

d. Le moment **où** il faut dire au revoir pour l'été n'est jamais facile.

e. Colin n'aime pas la salle **où** il fait très froid.

f. Béatrice a perdu le stylo **dont** elle a besoin pour son examen.

4.

a. Il y a **des** élèves qui parlent trop fort.

b. Elle n'a pas trouvé **de** livre (m.) sur son bureau.

c. J'ai besoin d'emprunter **une** gomme (f.)

d. L'institutrice a mis **des** affiches éducatives sur les murs.

e. Nous avons **un** examen (m.) demain matin.

f. La proviseure espère **de** bons résultats pour le brevet.

g. Ils ont laissé **une** chaise libre à côté de la porte.

h. On aborde beaucoup **de** sujets intéressants dans ce cours.

i. L'école fournit **un** ordinateur (m.) pour chaque élève.

j. Clarisse n'a pas **de** feuille blanche (f.) à te prêter.

Exercises III

1.

a. La mère de Faustine demande **si** sa fille rencontre des difficultés en sciences.

b. Le directeur précise **que** les bulletins sont envoyés par courrier.

c. Arthur demande **s'il** va avoir une réunion parents-professeurs la semaine prochaine.

d. Madame Durand dit **que** Paul fait des progrès remarquables en anglais.

e. Le père de Stéphane affirme **que** son fils a besoin de soutien scolaire.

f. Le secrétariat dit **que l'**on peut consulter les notes en ligne.

g. L'élève demande **s'**il peut toujours améliorer sa note en biologie.

h. Le professeur confirme **que** tous les élèves ont réussi l'examen.

i. La proviseure annonce **qu'**elle organise une réunion d'information.

j. La professeure demande à Marie **si** elles peuvent discuter après le cours.

2.

a. M. Flandrin demande aux élèves **s'ils ont** des questions.

b. Les parents disent **que leurs** enfants ne sont pas de mauvaises élèves.

c. La mère de Lucie demande **si sa fille travaille** bien en classe.

d. Le professeur demande aux collégiens **s'ils sont** capables de faire attention durant le cours.

e. Les lycéennes demandent **si elles** peuvent parler au conseiller d'orientation.

f. Le proviseur dit **que** les profs doivent rendre les notes avant le 26 juin.

3.

a. *Les étudiants sont...* It is most natural to complete this sentence with an adjective phrase.

For example: *Les étudiants sont <u>de plus en plus sérieux.</u>*

b. *Les professeurs veulent* ...It is most natural to complete this sentence with a noun phrase or a verb phrase.

For example: *Les professeurs veulent <u>de moins en moins de paperasse</u>* (paperwork) or *Les professeurs veulent <u>gagner de plus en plus</u>.*

c. *Les parents ont...* It is most natural to complete this sentence with a noun phrase.

For example: *Les parents ont <u>de plus en plus de demandes</u> / <u>de moins en moins de temps</u>.*

d. *Les enfants jouent...* It is most natural to complete this sentence with an adverb phrase.

For example: *Les enfants jouent <u>de moins en moins à l'extérieur</u> / <u>de plus en plus ensemble</u>.*

e. *Les salles de cours contiennent ...* It is most natural to complete this sentence with a noun phrase.

For example: *Les salles de cours contiennent <u>de plus en plus d'ordinateurs</u> / <u>de moins en moins de chaises vides</u>.*

f. *Les écoles enseignent...* It is most natural to complete this sentence with a noun phrase or an adverb phrase.

For example: *Les écoles enseignent <u>de plus en plus de langues étrangères</u>* or *Les écoles enseignent <u>de moins en moins formellement</u>.*

4.

a. Les étudiants sont **<u>souvent</u>** mécontents de leurs notes.
b. Mon professeur de français donne **<u>toujours</u>** des commentaires utiles.
c. Les profs donnent **<u>rarement</u>** des notes sans explications.
d. Le professeur de maths corrige nos devoirs **<u>tous les jours</u>**.
e. L'école organise **<u>régulièrement</u>** des réunions parents-professeurs.
f. Le proviseur **<u>ne</u>** critique **<u>jamais</u>** les professeurs en public.
g. Les parents demandent **<u>fréquemment</u>** des évaluations de progrès.
h. Les étudiants reçoivent des bulletins de notes **<u>tous les semestres</u>**.

5.

a. Les élèves **s'encouragent** avant l'examen.

b. Les parents d'élèves **se parlent** à la sortie de l'école.

c. Les professeurs **se motivent** pour rendre leurs carnets de notes à temps.

d. Sybille et moi **nous appelons** tous les soirs.

e. Toi et tes camarades de classe **vous vous soutenez** pendant les cours difficiles.

f. Il ne faut pas **se disputer** pour des bêtises.

g. M. Martin et Mme André **se croisent** dans le couloir.

h. Les proviseurs de l'académie **se félicitent** pour une année réussie.

6.

Citation (*Paul a dit : "Je vais aller à la bibliothèque après les cours."*)

Discours rapporté (*Marie m'a expliqué qu'il faut apporter des livres tous les jours.*)

Citation (*Le professeur a demandé : "Qui a fait les devoirs ?"*)

Discours rapporté (*Sophie a mentionné qu'ils vont apprendre l'histoire demain.*)

Citation (*"Il ne faut pas parler pendant la leçon," a insisté Mme Durand.*)

Discours rapporté (*Jean a raconté qu'ils ont une pause déjeuner d'une heure.*)

UNIT 3

Exercises I

1.

a. Les candidats **sont évalués** par le recruteur.

b. Mon CV **est mis à jour** par moi-même.

c. De nombreuses candidatures **sont reçues** par l'entreprise chaque jour.

d. Les entretiens d'embauche **sont passés** par Noah.

e. Nos prétentions salariales **sont concédées** par le cabinet.

f. Un poste d'informaticien **est recherché** par mon frère.

2.

a. On verse le salaire à la fin du mois.

b. Les compétences se perdent sans usage constant.

c. On présente une offre d'emploi après les entretiens réussis.

d. Aucune embauche ne se formalise pendant une grève.

e. On accepte sa demande d'augmentation.

f. Ma recherche de travail s'arrête pour l'été.

3.

a. sérieusement
b. clairement
c. prudemment
d. résolument
e. patiemment
f. précisément
g. agréablement
h. attentivement

4.

a. Mon patron est **moins compréhensif que** le tien.

b. Notre recherche avance **plus lentement que** l'on souhaite.

c. Ce stage est **aussi formateur que** mon précédent.

d. Ce poste exige quelqu'un **plus expérimenté que** lui.

e. Cette entreprise répond **moins vite que** les autres.

f. Ses qualifications sont **plus impressionnantes que** celles de l'autre candidat.

g. On peut se former **plus complètement** ici qu'ailleurs.
(Note the position of *que* is after the adverb of place *ici*.)

h. Cette nouvelle offre est **aussi attrayante que** l'ancienne.

Exercises II

1.

a. La lettre de motivation qu'elle a envoyée contient des fautes de frappe.

b. Les candidats que l'on a interviewés ne sont pas qualifiés.

c. Le CV que j'ai regardé est impressionnant.

d. A-t-il accepté l'offre ? Il l'a acceptée hier.

e. Le travail que j'ai fait dans ce poste est pertinent.

f. Pourquoi a-t-il quitté son dernier emploi ? Il l'a quitté à cause du salaire bas.

g. Les questions qu'ils ont posées sont très intimes.

h. Le recruteur vous a envoyé des fleurs. Je les ai mises (ou posées) sur votre bureau.

2.

a. <u>Comment gérez-vous le stress ?</u> Je gère le stress en prenant des pauses régulières.

b. <u>Pourquoi voulez-vous ce poste ?</u> Je veux ce poste parce qu'il correspond parfaitement à mes compétences.

c. <u>Que savez-vous de notre entreprise ?</u> Je sais que votre entreprise est un leader dans ce secteur.

d. <u>Où avez-vous travaillé après vos études ?</u> J'ai travaillé en Chine pendant deux ans après l'université.

e. <u>Quand voulez-vous commencer ?</u> J'aimerais commencer le 1er septembre.

3.

- a. *Nous devons vérifier vos références.*
- b. *Les chercheurs d'emploi peuvent obtenir des conseils gratuits.*
- c. *L'entreprise est obligée de divulguer les salaires.*
- d. *Les intervieweurs ne peuvent pas poser des questions au sujet de votre santé.*
- e. *Vous devez arriver à l'heure pour votre entretien.*

Exercises III

1.

- a. *Nous ne disposons __que__ de deux semaines pour répondre.*
- b. *Vous ne perdez __rien__ en acceptant cette offre.*
- c. *__Personne__ ne trouve la rémunération suffisante pour ces responsabilités.*
- d. *L'entreprise n'acceptera __jamais__ ces conditions.*
- e. *Les syndicats ne veulent __plus__ d'embauches en contrat à durée déterminée.*
- f. *Les stagiaires n'ont __plus__ la possibilité de travailler en alternance.*
- g. *Ils n'ont envoyé __personne__ pour négocier à leur place.*
- h. *__Rien__ ne pourrait remplacer les congés payés supprimés.*

2.

- a. *cependant*
- b. *malgré*
- c. *D'accord*
- d. *en même temps*
- e. *En revanche*

UNIT 4

Exercises I

1.

a. Les enfants **viennent d'**entrer dans un monde magique.

b. Le héros **est en train de** sauver la ville d'une invasion extraterrestre.

c. Les rebelles **sont en train de** préparer une attaque.

d. Les enquêteurs **viennent de** trouver un indice crucial.

e. Le pirate **est en train de** naviguer vers une île inconnue.

f. Le détective **vient de** rencontrer un témoin clé.

g. Le cambrioleur **vient de** voler les diamants.

h. Les aventuriers **sont en train de** découvrir un trésor caché.

i. Le scientifique **vient d'**avertir le président.

j. La princesse **est en train de** se libérer de la tour.

2. Double check your conjugation and vocabulary with a dictionary or translation tool.

Exercises II

1.

a. **En regardant** le match de rugby, il grignote.

b. **Après qu'ils terminent** l'entrainement, ils font des étirements.

c. **Avant d'aller** à la salle de sport, n'oublie pas de vérifier ton équipement.

d. **Pendant qu'il tire** un lancer-franc, les fans retiennent leur souffle.

e. **Après avoir nagé**, il se sèche avec une serviette.

f. **Pendant que nous jouons** au tennis, la pluie nous perturbe.

g. **Après avoir perdu** leur match, les handballeuses ont regardé l'enregistrement.

h. **Avant de lutter** au judo, nous nous saluons avec une révérence.

i. **En courant** de longues distances, elle écoute de la musique.

j. **Après avoir gagné** le tournoi, elles ont célébré avec leurs fans.

2.

a. Pendant la Coupe du monde, ils regardent les matchs **de midi à minuit**.

b. Le match de basket dure **jusqu'à 23h**.

c. Ils vont arriver au stade **dans cinq minutes**.

d. Le match de handball commence **à 20h**.

e. L'équipe commence son échauffement **vers 18h**.

f. **En hiver**, nous faisons souvent du ski alpin.

3.

a. La joueuse avec le numéro 12 sur son maillot est la plus rapide.

b. Les escrimeurs français frappent le plus précisément.

c. Ce joueur de tennis est le moins apprécié du tournoi.

d. Il joue le moins souvent de tous les joueurs de la ligue.

e. Les plongeurs chinois sont les plus gracieux de la compétition.

f. Le poids lourd est le boxeur le moins agile.

Exercises III

1.

a. Il a trouvé **quelques** points de crochet intéressants à essayer.

b. Elle a utilisé **une poignée de** boutons pour décorer son châle.

c. Avec **un brin de** couleur, le tableau va paraître moins sombre.

d. Il y a **un tas de** laines différentes dans cette boutique.

e. On peut utiliser **un bout de** tissu pour réparer ce trou.

f. Il nous faut **quelques** fermoirs pour les bracelets.

g. **Un brin de** fil doré peut embellir votre création.

h. Le couturier a mis **un morceau de** ruban pour une touche élégante.

i. Elle a besoin d'**un bout d'**éponge pour estomper les contours de l'aquarelle.

j. **Une pincée de** sable va ajouter du relief à votre tableau.

2.

a. Les aiguilles à tricoter sont **sur** l'étagère.

b. Le carton est **sous** la table de bricolage.

c. Les tissus sont **dans** l'armoire.

d. Le tableau est **devant** la fenêtre.

e. Les fournitures de bijouterie sont **près de** la porte.

f. Les pinceaux sont **derrière** les craies de couleurs.

g. La colle est **entre** les ciseaux et les boutons.

h. Le livre des patrons est **à côté de** la machine à coudre.

3.

Mon hobby préféré est la création de cadres en mosaïque. J'adore travailler avec des différentes couleurs et textures des tesselles. J'ai toujours **un tas de** vieilles assiettes **sur** ma table de travail.

Pour commencer, je choisis un cadre en bois et je casse **quelques** assiettes pour créer des tesselles uniques. Ensuite, je colle **un bout de** chaque couleur en utilisant une pince. Souvent, je dois chercher **une poignée de** morceaux cassés **dans** ma boîte à fournitures qui se trouve **sous** la table.

Les colles et mes outils sont toujours **à côté du** cadre, prêts à être utilisés. Parfois, j'ajoute **un brin de** paillettes pour donner un coup d'éclat. À la fin, je mets le cadre **près de** la fenêtre pour le faire sécher.

Créer des cadres en mosaïque est une activité relaxante et gratifiante pour moi.

Exercises IV

1.

a. vous aidiez

b. ils participent

c. je soutienne

d. nous contribuions

e. on organise

f. tu encourages

g. elles collectent

h. il distribue

i. nous sensibilisions

j. vous vous réunissiez

2.

a. *Il est évident que l'engagement des volontaires **aident** la communauté.* (Indicative)

b. *Est-il possible que nous **reportions** l'événement ?* (Subjunctive)

c. *Il est certain que la collecte de fonds **va** réussir cette année.* (Indicative)

d. *Elle n'est pas sûre que ce projet **soit** réalisable sans aide extérieure.* (Subjunctive)

e. *Je suis convaincue que tous les bénévoles **ressentent** beaucoup de satisfaction personnelle.* (Indicative)

f. *Pensez-vous que nous **ayons** assez de ressources pour lancer ce projet ?* (Subjunctive)

g. *Il est clair que l'association **fonctionne** grâce au soutien des membres.* (Indicative)

h. *Je doute que nous **puissions** organiser l'événement à temps.* (Subjunctive)

i. *Ils croient que leur association **fait** un travail remarquable.* (Indicative)

j. *Il est peu probable que chaque membre **comprenne** les statuts.* (Subjunctive)

UNIT 5

Exercises I

1.

a. elles jouaient
b. tu courrais
c. je sautais
d. nous nagions
e. il riait
f. vous dessiniez
g. on rêvait
h. elle explorait
i. ils se déguisaient
j. tu construisais

2.

a. J'ai gagné au football hier.
b. Il regardait des dessins animés chaque matin.
c. Tu es tombé de ton vélo l'été dernier.
d. J'ai appris à jouer à cache-cache ce matin.
e. Nous rendions visite à nos grands-parents chaque été.
f. Vous avez joué dans le bac à sable la semaine dernière.
g. Elle peignait chaque après-midi.
h. Ils grimpaient toujours sur la cage à poule pendant la récréation.
i. Nous faisions voler des cerfs-volants à la plage.
j. On adorait jouer à chat perché avec mes cousins.

3.

a. Il regrette de dire des méchancetés à ses amis.
b. Je regrette de ne pas avoir étudié plus pendant le lycée / quand j'étais au lycée.
c. Regrettes-tu d'être resté dans ta ville d'enfance ?
d. Nous regrettons d'avoir déménagé aux banlieues.
e. Vous n'allez pas regretter d'acheter ce livre.
f. Ils regrettaient de ne pas s'être couchés plus tôt.

Exercises II

1.

a. *ils décideront*

b. *j'investirai*

c. *le marché augmentera*

d. *nous lancerons*

e. *vous préparerez*

f. *tu organiseras*

g. *elle développera*

h. *les ventes atteindront*

i. *on verra*
(Note: This is a very common response when someone does not want to commit to a future plan. "We'll see.")

j. *vous ferez*

Exercises III

1.

a. *vous voyageriez*
b. *elle achèterait*
c. *ils iraient*
d. *nous créerions*
e. *tu réussirais*
f. *je découvrirais*
g. *on aurait*
h. *il travaillerait*
i. *elles seraient*
j. *nous étudierions*

2.

a. *Nous aurions aimé travailler ensemble.*

b. *Ils seraient allés en France pour les vacances.*

c. *Tu aurais eu une carrière impressionnante.*

d. *Elle serait restée plus longtemps avec plus d'argent.*

e. *Avec un meilleur guide, vous auriez vu tous les monuments.*

f. *J'aurais adoré découvrir de nouveaux horizons.*

g. *Ils auraient été très fiers de leur fille.*

h. *Tu serais devenu un grand artiste à une autre époque.*

i. *Sans la capitaine, elles auraient perdu tous les matchs.*

j. *Je serais sorti plus souvent.*

3. Double check your conjugation and vocabulary with a dictionary or translation tool.

MORE BOOKS BY LINGO MASTERY

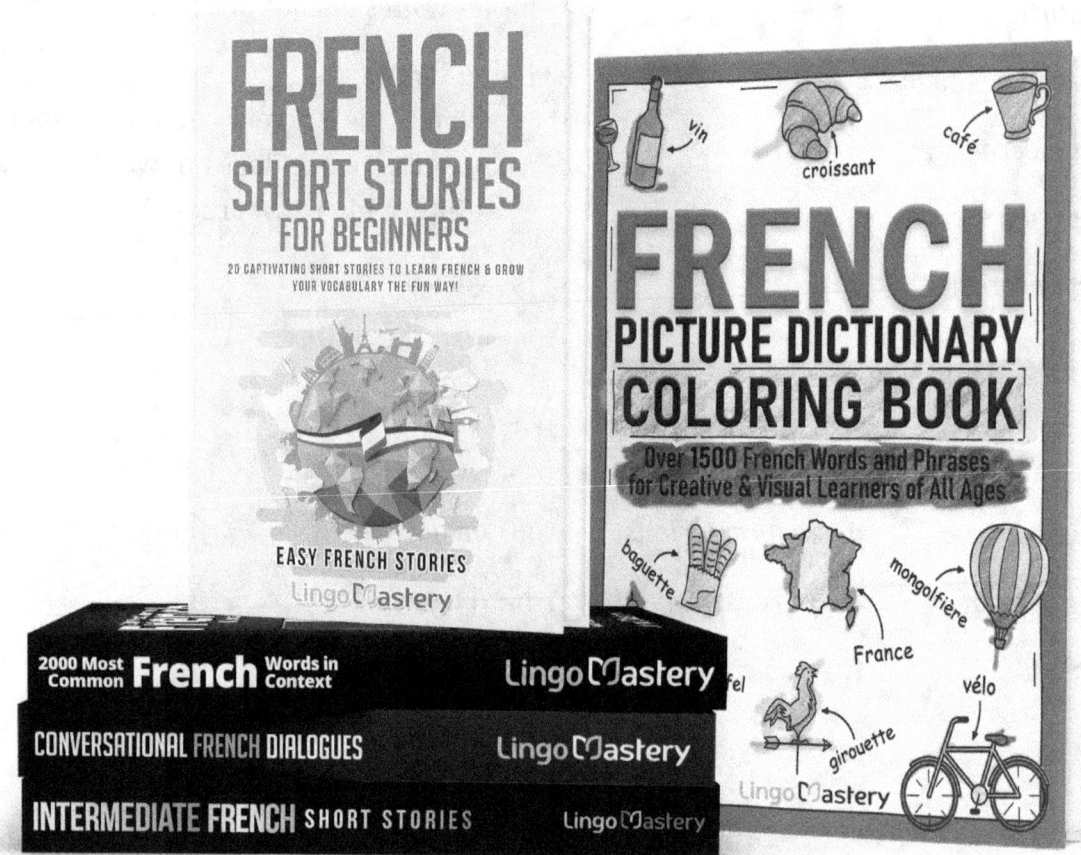

We are not done teaching you French until you're fluent!

Here are some other titles you might find useful in your journey of mastering French:

✓ French Short Stories for Beginners

✓ Intermediate French Short Stories

✓ 2000 Most Common French Words in Context

✓ Conversational French Dialogues

But we have many more!

Check out all of our titles at www.lingomastery.com/french

www.ingramcontent.com/pod-product-compliance
Lightning Source LLC
Chambersburg PA
CBHW081444070526
44586CB00019B/2223